ood Americana, David Page gives a hungry public just what it needs: ascinating inside scoop on our nation's most iconic foods, and the ons why they are so beloved. Page's rich storytelling sets a grand , serves a literary feast, and leaves you savoring every morsel."

—Adrian Miller, James Beard Award-winning author of
*Soul Food: The Surprising Story of an American Cuisine, One
Plate at a Time*

 people think about the background and staying power of the favorite s they eat. David Page brings each food's history to every bite!"

—Marvin Lender, cofounder of Lender's Frozen Bagels

elicious, nutritious multi-course meal of history that goes down as easy appetizer, but satisfies like a main course."

—Gustavo Arellano, author of *Taco USA: How Mexican Food
Conquered America*

ood Americana, David Page celebrates America's iconic dishes: what are, where they came from, where they are going, who loves them, why. It's a gold mine of information, told not just with facts, but with iling anecdotes and good humor. This is a book that shows how deeply brilliantly (and deliciously) what we eat defines who we are."

—Michael Stern, author of *Roadfood*

Praise for
Food Americana

"Terrific food journalism. Page uncovers the untold backs
American food. A great read."

—George Stephanopoulos, coanchor of *Good*
host of *This Week*, and chief an

"*Food Americana* dives deep into the history, subculture, an
everyone's favorite foods. It's an incredible read."

—Tony Gemignani, thirteen-time World

"A delicious swirl of entertaining stories to fulfill any food

—Jerry Greenfield, cofoun

"Every food, regardless of time and place, ingredients, or m
preparation, has a history. David Page offers a breathtaking
time, guiding us to the stories behind the foods we eat."

—Hasia Diner, program director at New Yor
author of *Hung*

"An original gem. David Page has written a humorous cultu
of deep research, smart anecdotes, novel information, and m
accounts of the origins of our favorite foods. I didn't know h
goes into a taco."

—Martin Fletcher, TV correspondent and
Book Award-winning author of

FOOD AMERICANA

FOOD AMERICANA

*The Remarkable
People and Incredible
Stories behind America's
Favorite Dishes*

DAVID PAGE

mango
PUBLISHING GROUP

CORAL GABLES

Published by Mango Publishing Group, a division of Mango Media Inc.

Cover, Layout & Design: Morgane Leoni
Cover Illustration: © lukeruk / Adobe Stock

For permission requests, please contact the publisher at:

Mango Publishing Group
2850 S Douglas Road, 2nd Floor
Coral Gables, FL 33134 USA
info@mango.bz

For special orders, quantity sales, course adoptions and corporate sales, please email the publisher at sales@mango.bz. For trade and wholesale sales, please contact Ingram Publisher Services at: customer.service@ingramcontent.com or +1.800.509.4887.

Food Americana: The Remarkable People and Incredible Stories behind America's Favorite Dishes

Library of Congress Cataloging-in-Publication number: 2021931802
ISBN: (p) 978-1-64250-586-3, (e) 978-1-64250-587-0
BISAC category code CKB030000, COOKING / Essays & Narratives

Printed in the United States of America

For Roberta.

For a million wonderful reasons.

Contents

Preface

When I was a child, my grandmother used to make me something she, for some reason, called Jewish spaghetti. It was pasta, boiled, then fried in a pan with onions and ketchup. And yes, it was as awful as it sounds. But in its own way, it is a perfect example of how America created a cuisine: a Jewish woman, who came to this country to escape the violent anti-Semitism of pre-World-War-Two Poland, cooking some version of an Italian dish that she saw as an American staple. The history of American food is the story of embracing another country's cuisine, then changing it. And, as one of those who lives to eat instead of eating to live, I have long been fascinated by the backstories of food. How did a dish come to be? In making *Diners, Drive-Ins and Dives*, I focused on individual plates. Individual people. And I realized that virtually all of these classic American food stories had one thing in common—they began someplace else. So, I decided to tell the broader story, how America imported the cuisines of many different countries and combined them into a cuisine of our own. I began in late 2018, talking to academics, experts, and many, many restaurateurs. Halfway through (after my reporting on large group events, such as the Buffalo Chicken Wing Festival, had been completed), the COVID-19 pandemic hit, and within its overall tragedy, it had a major impact on the restaurant business. Many employees were laid off or fired. Many restaurants went out of business entirely. Even the most high-end restaurants began doing takeout to survive. Americans had to rethink something as basic as how to eat. Yet, the essence of our cuisine did not change—the pizza we had delivered, the breakfast bagel from a drive-through, the grab-and-go-sushi purchased during a quick, masked visit to the convenience store—all are examples of food from elsewhere that we now call our own. This is their story. And ours.

American Pie

I'm sweating miserably. My left hand feels like it's on fire, which makes sense since I've shoved it into a thousand-degree oven to maneuver a long metal pole with a perforated oversized spatula on the end. It's a pizza peel, used to move the pies around as they bake between searing hot coals on the left and intense gas flames on the right. And I'm feeling every one of the thousand degrees as I try, again and again, to get the pizzas just right. It turns out, you don't just slide one in, wait a few minutes, then slide it out. No, you've got to start by charring the crust and turning the pizza as each section facing the fire blackens just enough. Then, after each turn, the pizza must return to the exact same spot it was on, which has cooled a bit from heating the crust. Any part that lands on the hotter area outside that circle will burn, and I'm having a hell of a time, not just landing in the right place, but turning the pies in the first place. I'm at Tony Gemignani's International School of Pizza, and it appears I'm not one of the smart kids.

Gemignani is one of the leading lights in the world of pizza, the first American to be named World Champion Pizza Maker at the World Pizza Cup in Naples, where pizza was born, and the winner of more than a dozen other pizza competition championships. He has welcomed me to join one of the classes he teaches out of his Pizza Napolitana restaurant in the traditionally Italian North Beach neighborhood of San Francisco. This is before the COVID pandemic, and applications are way up, he says, because more and more novices want to learn how to make pizza, and more and more established pizza makers want to learn how to make it better.

"There is a renaissance now in pizza," he says. "Everything's evolving, the ingredients are evolving. It has been for the last ten years, especially with chefs coming into our industry, with bakers coming into our industry and making pizza great again."

Again? Pizza is arguably already Americans' favorite food. There are nearly seventy-eight thousand pizza restaurants in the country. Three billion pizzas sold a year. That's twenty-three pounds for each of us. A forty-six-billion dollar a year business domestically. But Gemignani is talking about more than sales figures. He's talking about growing consumer interest in more than delivery from Domino's. The chains account for 60 percent of pizza sales, leaving 40 percent for independent restaurant owners, who are focusing increasingly on quality, artisanship, and different regional styles, in many cases, because the market demands it. "The consumer now is a little smarter," Gemignani says. "They're willing to take chances versus your old faithfuls." This is true not only in the big, food-focused cities like New York and Chicago.

My pizza school classmate Hope Dadah is betting it is time for a change in Rapid City, South Dakota, where she and her parents run a pizzeria that has been selling only New York style pizza for thirty years. "No one really taught us how to do it," she says. "Just a lot of trial and error. And then we just kind of let it grow. Lots of practice, though. Lots of pizza-eating." But now, she says, it's time for a change. "We'd like to maybe expand to a different restaurant and bring Neapolitan to Rapid City," she says, "Because obviously that's not something that's in South Dakota right now." So, she is here in class, learning how to make the signature pizza of pizza's signature city, Naples. Says Gemignani, "What's old is new again."

Old as in ancient. There is archeological evidence of multiple civilizations baking flatbreads thousands of years ago. Some argue that pizza was brought to Italy by the Greeks. And the first reference to the actual word "pizza" in Italy was in 997 AD. Centuries later, evolving from flatbread, pizza became a staple food of the poor in Naples, with such basic toppings as garlic, lard, and salt. Pizza topped with cheese and tomato sauce, pizza marinara, did not appear until the eighteenth century. In the nineteenth century, it came to America with a flood of Southern Italian immigrants fleeing poverty. Carol Helstosky, who teaches at the University of Denver and wrote *Pizza: A Global History* says, "When pizza goes from Italy to New York, it's still food for the poor. It's for poor workers. It's sold so that they could take it, usually, to work on a busy day. It's portable."

At first it was made in bakeries, alongside the bread and rolls, but eventually, establishments making only pizza, called pizzerias, appeared. For decades, the first documented pizzeria was said to be Lombardi's in New York in 1905. The claim is emblazoned in the tiles above their oven today. But statistician and pizza fanatic Peter Regas, who exhaustively researched the subject, recently uncovered evidence of a pizzeria operating in 1894, an establishment called Forno E Pizzeria, Italian for "Oven and Pizzeria," a name that Regas found hidden away in the baker's section of an 1894 business directory. And it is quite possible there were others in business even earlier.

Whoever came first, the pizza business in New York and a handful of other cities with Italian immigrant populations grew steadily from the start of the twentieth century. The pizzas were Neapolitan, the ones the proprietors knew from home, but they weren't quite the same. Pizza historian Scott Wiener says, "The New York style was birthed from applying the method of Naples to the ingredients and technology of America." There was no other option. Pizza ovens in Naples burned wood. Ovens in New York were larger and burned coal. That required a longer bake time and, combined with America's higher protein wheat, created a crisper, less chewy crust. And it was impossible to get mozzarella from Italy, since it would spoil on the eleven-day transatlantic boat trip, so domestic mozzarella, not quite the same, had to be used instead. But what they created out of necessity was remarkable, and New York-style pizza remains widely popular today.

For the first half of the century, pizza slowly spread across the rest of the country. Then it took off. "You begin to see pizza exploding in popularity in the 1950s," says Helstosky. Dean Martin was singing, "When the moon hits your eye like a big pizza pie, that's amore." Pizzerias proliferated for the first time outside of traditional Italian neighborhoods, even in small towns, a development made possible by the invention of the gas-fired pizza oven.

But the most important step in pizza conquering America was the vision of a handful of entrepreneurs with no Italian connection and no pizza expertise, just plenty of business sense. Helstosky explains, "The popularity of pizza in the rest of the United States had much more to do with the rise of pizza franchises, in particular Pizza Hut and Domino's, which starts off as DomiNick's, both of which appear at the end of the 1950s," she says. "Those, I think, had significant impact for the way that they produce and sell pizza, and that makes it truly a family-friendly food to eat."

The chains would create a new American, and far less Italian, style of pizza—a crisper crust, much heavier on the sauce and toppings, replacing fresh ingredients with longer-shelf-life processed items, and bringing a uniformity, a sameness to pizza in state after state. It began in the Midwest, where the market was wide open. Brothers Frank and Dan Carney opened the first Pizza Hut in 1958 in Wichita, Kansas. Little Caesar's began in 1959 in Garden City, Michigan. Domino's began in Ypsilanti, Michigan, in 1960. Today, there are more than a hundred chains in America, ranging in size from a handful of outlets to Pizza Hut's more than eighteen thousand locations worldwide. (They have the most units, but Domino's beats them in revenue, almost sixteen billion dollars to a little more than twelve billion dollars in 2018.)

A key element was delivery. The chains didn't invent it—the mom-and-pops offered it first, some as early as the 1930s—but it was the chains that brought it to millions. "The chains made it commonplace," says pizza historian Scott Wiener. "They made it so everybody had to offer it who wasn't already offering it."

They expanded quickly, capitalizing on America's growing embrace of franchising, soon becoming the standard for millions of Americans. They would even become ubiquitous in areas where pizza was a tradition and had been long before the chains came along. For the next few decades, pizza didn't really change much. The chains continued to grow. And new immigrants continued opening independent pizzerias, though many now came from Greece, not Italy. Pizza had become one of America's favorite foods, an everyday option. Don't want to leave home? There's delivery. Want to go out but not dress up? What's more casual than a pizzeria? Watching your wallet with a family to feed? Nothing's cheaper than pizza.

But pizza today is far more than delivery or an everyday pie. It is a staple at white tablecloth and even upscale restaurants known for their remarkable culinary creations. Alice Waters features pizza in the upstairs café at her famed Chez Panisse restaurant in Berkeley, where the aroma of the wood-burning pizza oven suffuses the room. Waters is a culinary legend, a pioneer—possibly even the creator— of the farm-to-table movement. Every pizza she serves is made almost entirely of locally grown, organic ingredients. Recently, they've been serving a cured anchovy and tomato sauce pizza with hot pepper; one with goat cheese, mozzarella, herbs, and prosciutto; another with wild mushrooms and green garlic. Waters says, "It's so about ingredients, and where they come from for me. And so, we're doing a pizza which is very surprising right now. And it has been for the last year, but our farmer started sending us nettles. And we started playing around with cooking them, because they're incredibly nutritious. And we cook them with garlic, olive oil, and they have become a favorite pizza at Chez Panisse because nobody can believe you can eat stinging nettles."

For Waters, it all began with a trip to Europe. "On our way to Switzerland with my friends for Thanksgiving, we stopped in Torino," she says. "And because there was this fire that we saw through the window (of a local restaurant). And they were making pizzas. And we just stopped the car and went in there. And it was so warm and so beautiful. And I said, 'Oh, my God, we could do this at Chez Panisse.' " That was more than forty years ago. And it opened the floodgates to a world of creative pizza we now take for granted.

Waters actually inspired celebrity chef Wolfgang Puck to buy a pizza oven when he opened Spago in Beverly Hills. Today, having built an international restaurant empire, Puck is still best known for his smoked salmon pizza with crème fraiche. It's on the menu at Spago in Beverly Hills. And Spago in Istanbul. And seemingly wherever *Entertainment Tonight* covers Puck catering a Hollywood A-list awards party. And it is gorgeous. The glistening, house-cured smoked salmon, sliced perfectly thin. The bright white crème fraiche peeking out from underneath. Heaping ovals of black salmon roe at the center of each slice. And the edge of the crust, properly irregular, with just the right amount of char.

And it was Puck's wildly creative pizza chef, Ed LaDou, who made nontraditional pizza available nationally, when he went on to create the menu for the California Pizza Kitchen chain, most notably featuring barbecued chicken pizza, which has since become a menu standard at chains and independent pizzerias all over the country. "Experimentation is always good for pizza," says Scott Wiener, even though he still prefers a more traditional pie. "Every single day, I get the question, 'What do you think about pineapple on pizza? Should they put the pickles on the pizza?' Now there's this kiwi pizza picture on the internet that people seem to think is important. Like every single day, and the fact that it keeps hitting the conversation, that it's so relevant, it means that it's good for pizza."

Yet, the hottest trend in pizza these days is a return to the past. It's called artisanal pizza, baked in wood-fired ovens, with fresh local ingredients, dough crafted carefully from the best flour, and everything done by hand. Prominent among the artisanal styles is an homage to pizza's beginnings, Neapolitan. Unlike traditional New York pizza, which is sturdy enough to fold over and often piled with toppings, authentic Neapolitan is more pillowy, and topped with no more than crushed tomatoes, cheese, and basil. Tony Gemignani, who offers a course in Neapolitan pizza at his International Pizza School says, "True Neapolitan pizza is charred, chewy, wet, soupy. A soupy Neapolitan is common. Sometimes people go to Naples and say, 'Everything is sloppy here.' Or 'It's the best pizza I ever had in my life.' It's one or the other."

And it's fragile. "If you haven't eaten it in like two minutes, I'm cringing," he says. "If you haven't eaten it in five minutes, you guys are talking about something, I'm pissed." He says if Neapolitan pizza is not eaten immediately, it degrades so badly that it shouldn't be eaten at all. "A lot of times I'll say, 'Hey, just take this pizza away from them. Take it away, I'm going to make him a new one. Tony wants you to have a new one,' because it sits. It doesn't hold well. Any pizza that's cooked in sixty seconds is not a pizza that's going to stay warm long."

There are only two kinds of "authentic" Neapolitan pizza—marinara, topped simply with tomatoes and mozzarella made from cow's milk, and Margherita, with tomatoes, mozzarella, and fresh basil. In pizza school, Tony had each of us make a Margherita. Precisely and carefully. Stretching the dough to just the right thickness. Placing the basil leaves shiny side up, even though they would each be hidden by a chunk of mozzarella. Sliding the pizza peel under the thin dough was nowhere near as easy as it looked, nor was dropping it into the oven—I apparently "shoveled" it in, landing in the wrong spot with only a minute to work with before it burned. And there was even more that had to be done just right—turning it repeatedly until the crust showed the proper amount of charred spots called leoparding, without burning, returning it to the exact same spot after each turn to keep it from burning, lifting the pizza up above the fire to finish the bottom of the crust. Again, all of this happens in little more than a minute. Tony acknowledged that for a beginner, this was a tough test. "Neapolitan's very hard," he says. "It's nerve-wracking. When people do it, they're like 'I want to do it,' then they're like, 'I don't know if I can do this every day.' "

Perhaps the most influential force in artisanal pizza is in, of all places, Phoenix, Arizona. Former New Yorker Chris Bianco opened Pizzeria Bianco there in 1994, and he has been making transcendent pizza in a wood-fired oven ever since from homemade mozzarella and the finest ingredients, often locally grown, some even on the pizzeria's property. He's been acclaimed over the years by food writer after food writer as making the best pizza in America. "I don't know about that," he says modestly. "It's so subjective. Who's the cutest puppy or who's got the best pizza? I think what I've always tried to do is, no matter what situation I'm in, I'll make it better than I found it."

And even though writers have talked about Pizzeria Bianco's Neapolitan-style pizza, Bianco says in reality it isn't. "I studied Neapolitan pizza and I respect it so much that I knew I wasn't from Naples," he says. "My family was from Puglia and I was born in the Bronx. So, it might serve me best to be my authentic self. And I could honestly say, 'Neapolitan isn't my favorite.' It doesn't mean it's not the greatest. It's not my favorite only because I like it a little crisper. I might not like it so loose in the middle."

So, he adjusted bake time, temperature, hydration, and even the protein level in his flour to achieve "something that's maybe more like you'd see in Puglia where they do a little bit lower temperature. Or even in Rome where you'll see a little bit crisper," and reminiscent of the pizza he grew up with in the Bronx. He describes it as, "that strong, toothy New York style married with the quick bake of a wood fire."

There are only six pizzas on Bianco's menu, unchanged from the day he opened. There's the Margherita, with tomato sauce, fresh mozzarella and basil; Marinara, with tomato sauce, oregano, and garlic, but no cheese; the Sonny Boy, with tomato sauce, mozzarella, salami, and olives; the Rosa, with red onion, Parmigiano-Reggiano, rosemary, and pistachios; the Biancoverde, with mozzarella, Parmigiano-Reggiano, ricotta, and arugula; and the Wiseguy, with wood-roasted onion, smoked mozzarella, and fennel sausage. All with just the right amount of leoparding around the raised edges of the crust and served, bubbling, within seconds of being taken from the oven.

Pizza fanatics constantly come to Phoenix just to try one. Or several. Daryl and Mindi Hirsch, who have traveled the world eating and writing about their experiences on their *2foodtrippers* blog, brought great expectations with them. "We hear all this hype," Daryl says. "And I'm like, 'okay, I hope they're not disappointing,' because we did a detour. And sure enough, the pizza was amazing. It was really great. What was really unique about these pies is, he took a really Italian approach, which is using the freshest stuff that's available locally and it really did translate to the flavors of the pizza. We had a wonderful pie with basil. And there was also a really wonderful sausage pie. I remember his sausage was made fresh in house. It was really fantastic."

And it isn't just foodies who make the pilgrimage. Other pizza makers do too, hoping to learn Chris Bianco's "secrets," which he willingly shares. "I talked to a lot of pizza makers over the years," he says. "And I tend to preface advice with one caveat, and that being that there's no gospel to this work, not to what I'm going to tell you. I can only tell you about my experience and I hope that helps you shape the way you see things and I hope, if I've raised the bar, that you dance on that bar one day. And you raise that bar."

The message has gotten out. Not just from Bianco, but from other talented artisanal pizza makers as well. No, most pizzeria owners will not grow their own toppings. Or make their own cheese. But more and more are raising their standards. Using better ingredients. Learning the chemistry of making dough. Exploring the history of the kind of pizza they want to make. Like Tony Cerimele, who owns New Columbus Pizza Co. in Nesquehoning, Pennsylvania, near Scranton. "You're seeing a lot more of people like myself and independent guys changing how we make dough," he says. "Changing what we offer, using better ingredients. Using top notch stuff that we weren't doing five, six, seven, eight, nine, ten years ago."

Cerimele specializes in something called Old Forge pizza, invented in the nearby town of Old Forge, Pennsylvania, to feed hungry coal miners back in 1926. It's a pan pizza baked with a combination of cheeses that often includes processed American. The crust, which looks imposing, is surprisingly light. There are two choices— red, with tomato sauce on top of the cheese; and white, which sandwiches the cheese between two layers of dough. Today, there are so many restaurants serving both in Old Forge—as many as a dozen, five in a little more than a block on Main Street—that the town of eight thousand people has declared itself the pizza capital of the world. And as unique as it may be, Old Forge is just one of many homegrown pizza styles that have long been unique to particular regions.

Steve Green, publisher of pizza industry trade publication *PMQ Pizza Magazine* says, "You've got the whole US, this jungle, this rain forest of pizza operators out there, and in some areas, they've created markets where somebody came up with a good idea, and then a competitor started copying their idea, and pretty soon you had a bunch of customers that liked it. And so, we're blessed with probably twenty different regional styles in the US that are all great." And the next step in the pizza renaissance seems to be the impending "discovery" of all of them by a new audience." Tony Gemignani says, "Seeing pictures beautified on Instagram, and seeing this style, and having it in front of you on your phone every freaking minute of the day. It definitely makes you want to try it."

And there is so much to try. There's St. Louis pizza, thin and crisp and topped with provel cheese, a processed combination of Swiss, provolone, cheddar and liquid smoke; New Haven style, baked in a coal oven, crunchy, chewy, and often topped with clams; Ohio Valley style, with all toppings added after baking; A trio from Chicago—deep dish, stuffed, and thin crust; Quad Cities style, with a sweet crust topped with fennel sausage and a spicy sauce. And there's grilled pizza in Rhode Island, grandma pizza, Philadelphia tomato pie, not to be confused with Trenton tomato pie, New York style, Brooklyn style, Midwest style, New England Greek style, and Buffalo style, with cup-and-char pepperoni that crisps and curls up around a puddle of grease as it cooks. And one that in the last few years has rocketed to national popularity after six decades of anonymity: Detroit-style. It's a rectangular pan pizza, perhaps most notable for a rim of caramelized cheese all around the edges. The dough is extremely thick but surprisingly light, crunchy yet pillowy.

Created in 1946 by Detroit bar owner Gus Guerra, who initially baked them in heavy, blue-steel industrial pans "liberated" by friends from an auto plant or shop, Detroit pizza was virtually unknown outside of Michigan until Shawn Randazzo, owner of the aptly named Detroit Style Pizza Co. in suburban Detroit, did something remarkable. He won the most prestigious pizza competition in America—and one of the most prestigious in the world—the International Pizza Challenge in Las Vegas. "Everyone kept on saying, 'You've got to go to Vegas. You've got to go to Vegas and compete,' " he told me. "So, I went there in 2012, and I won World Champion Pizza Maker of the year, and then that got a lot of exposure to this style of pizza."

Suddenly, pizza makers from all over the country wanted to make this pizza they'd never heard of before, in Austin, Denver, New York, all across the country. *Esquire* ran an article online entitled "Hip to Be Square: Detroit-Style Pizza Is Conquering America." The pizza renaissance is erasing regional boundaries as people search for the next great thing. Tony Gemignani, who has had Detroit-style pizza on his menu for several years, says, "Detroit's hot right now, grandma pizzas are hot right now, tavern style pizza's hot right now, Roman style pizza's hot right now. What will be the new hot thing after all this?"

Some of the new hot things aren't styles, they're trends, picking up traction across the industry, such as pizza marketed as healthier—cauliflower crust, gluten free, keto. There's technology, big chains relying on ordering apps, especially to attract Generation Z, consumers born after 1996. There's also the target market for an entirely new category of pizza restaurant, combining elements of artisanal pizza, chain pizza, and "healthy" pizza. These growing "fast casual" chains, such as MOD Pizza, Pieology, Pie Five Pizza, and Blaze Pizza emphasize fresh ingredients, health, high-tech quick-cooking ovens, and the opportunity for customers to pick their own toppings as they walk down an ordering line. Based on the Chipotle model, the idea is to combine speed with quality. Rick Wetzel, who founded Blaze with his wife, Elise—they previously created the Wetzel's Pretzels chain—says, "We speak to Gen Z. That's who we are, and all of our restaurants play college alt-rock music. They're a little edgy. We keep the music a little loud." And he says, "We consider ourselves a lifestyle brand and not a food brand. We don't expect people to stand up and say, 'Hey, let's go for pizza. Where do you want to go?' We expect people to stand up and say, 'Hey, let's go to Blaze.' "

In 2017, *Forbes* named Blaze the fastest growing chain ever. Basketball superstar LeBron James is such a fan that he became a franchisee, bought an estimated 10 percent of the company, and dumped a fifteen-million-dollar guaranteed endorsement deal with McDonalds to become Blaze's commercial spokesman. Wetzel says they're gunning for the big chains, such as Domino's. "It's going to take some time," he acknowledges, since Blaze still has just a few more than three hundred locations. But, he says, "You look at what Starbucks did to Maxwell House and Folgers and look what Uber did to the taxicab industry or Netflix did to Blockbuster. People love disruptive brands these days."

Yet for all that's new, much of America's love for pizza is rooted in history, nostalgia, and comfort, and not just in places like New York or Chicago. Tom Bordenaro opened a pizzeria on the south side of Des Moines, Iowa, in 1977. His son Chris runs it today, in the same way his father did. "We're not the blah pizza places that don't have any flavor to their pizza," he says. "We're known for thin crust and spicy sauce, everything's made in house." "It's a homestyle pizza," says Danny Van Syoc at the bar getting some beers with a friend after work and enjoying his beef, bacon, and mushroom pizza. "It's not Papa John's, it's not Pizza Hut," he says. "And the atmosphere here is very neighborhood. And that's what I like the most about it is you come here, it's almost like *Cheers* for a pizza place. You get to know the cooks back there, you wave at them when you come in. The owner, he comes out, 'Hey, how you doing?' "

The signature pie here is named for Chris Bordenaro's father Tom, who was known as Bordy. "It's called the Bordy's Special," he says. "It has eight toppings on it. Sausage, pepperoni, capicola, beef, black olives, green peppers, onions, and mushrooms." Travis Young, waiting for his carry-out order, says it's the only pizza he ever gets. "I used to come here with my grandparents," he says. "It's what my grandparents got, it's what we always get." And it's what he is getting again today.

Travis Young is able to relive his memories because Bordenaro's is keeping tradition alive. So is Frank & Helen's pizzeria in suburban St. Louis. Vito & Nick's in Chicago. Terita's in Columbus, Ohio. Tommaso's in San Francisco. Totonno's on Coney Island. And countless others in countless cities and towns all across the country. Serving up their version of the dish that, over two hundred years, has become a classic American food. Bordenaro sums it up with a simple truth: "I don't know one person who doesn't like pizza."

Tony Gemignani's Grandma Sausage & Pepperoni Pizza

Ingredients

- 12 x 12 inch grandma or Sicilian pizza pan with edge
- 2½ oz. olive oil
- 18 oz. dough (purchased from local pizzeria or supermarket)
- Nine 1 oz. slices whole milk mozzarella
- One 4 oz. fresh mozzarella, sliced
- ¼ oz. grated Parmigiano-Reggiano cheese
- 5 oz. hand-crushed tomatoes, strained
- 3 oz. tomato sauce of choice
- 0.25–0.3 oz. basil chiffonade
- a pinch of sea salt and black pepper
- 1½ oz. sliced cup-n-char pepperoni or sliced pepperoni
- 3 oz. Italian sausage pinched into flat dime-size pieces
- garlic oil drizzle

Directions

- Pour 1½ oz. olive oil into a pan. Cover and coat both sides of the dough in olive oil. Make sure the entire inside of the pan is also coated with a light amount of oil. Place dough into the pan, push it out to the ends, and let it rest for 1 hour in a warm area. Gently re-push the dough out to the corners of the pan. Dimple the dough with your fingertips.

- Place the oven rack on the middle level. Place a stone or pizza steel on the rack. Pre-heat the oven to bake at 500–550 degrees. When the oven is at temperature, place the pizza on the surface and bake it for 5 to 6 minutes. During this time, slightly warm tomato sauce on the stove top and set that aside.

- Using a spatula, carefully take the par-baked pizza out of the oven. Add the remaining 1 oz. of olive oil around the sides of the inner pan. Evenly place sliced mozzarella cheese on top, leaving a quarter-inch border. Add crushed tomato, pepperoni, and pinched Italian sausage, and return the pizza to the oven and finish baking until it's golden brown. Remove the pizza from the oven. Slice. Top it with sauce, diagonally striped. Place sliced fresh mozzarella over the sauce lines. Finish with salt, pepper, oregano, Parmigiano-Reggiano, basil, and garlic oil.

Mexican Food in America—A Tale of Two Cuisines

They built a shrine in the darkness at the site of their loss. Some brought candles. Others brought flowers. Some raised lighters and phones as if at a concert. As many as two or three hundred people came together to say goodbye to a dear friend—the Taco Bell in downtown State College, Pennsylvania. The restaurant, one of the few three-in-the-morning options for Penn State University students after a night of drinking, had shut down without notice just five days earlier. "It was almost surreal," says Penn State senior Michael Sneff, who was at the vigil reporting for the student newspaper. "It was cold that night," he says. "It was March first, and it was in the low twenties and people are out there with candles and flowers and signs. It was insane." At one point, many in the crowd linked arms and swayed to the Penn State Alma Mater.

The organizer of the vigil, Prajesh Patel, a senior, addressed the crowd while wearing a taco costume. "Taco Bell was our home away from home and added spice to our life," he said, adding, "Life isn't fair." And for many of those who attended, the night became far more emotional than they expected. "Initially, it was a joke. It was a meme," Sneff says. "But it developed into a lot more than that. I think it was a thing where the majority of people showed up thinking it was a joke, such as myself. Then they stayed and honestly, we're not allowed to be biased in our reporting actually, but I found the scene very moving. I know it sounds ridiculous, but I mean that Taco Bell was really special to a lot of students, I found out." And he says, "When people started bringing speakers and playing that Sarah McLachlan song 'In the Arms of an Angel' and people started holding up their candles, you can't not be moved. It was honestly just surreal and crazy."

Junior D. J. Krause said, "Legends were made at this Taco Bell, you've got to come to pay your respects." Senior Noah Yudt said, "I can't tell you how many times I've come here at one thirty in the morning, just hungry after a night out." Sneff summed it up as, "just the perfect storm of everything that students could possibly want. It was cheap, it was open late nights, and it gets you that craving that you want of Mexican food and tacos. There's nothing like sitting in a crowded Taco Bell at three thirty in the morning when you're buzzed and shoving a Doritos taco in your face for a lot of students."

And there were a handful of brief references to the food. But not many. Kevin Victor, a junior, told the crowd that while the Taco Bell was now gone, "It lives here, in our sauce packets." Organizer Patel told them, "I'm gonna miss the taste of that crunchy taco and chicken chalupa." But it was clear that most were mourning the loss of a familiar late-night hangout, far more than the loss of great Mexican food, even if any believed that is what their Taco Bell served. Almost certainly unknown to the vigil-goers, however, was the pivotal role Taco Bell played in making Mexican food an American staple.

It began with one man, Glen Bell, who entered the fast-food business in 1948 with a hot dog and hamburger stand in San

Bernardino, California, near where the first McDonald's would open four years later. He took to eating at Mexican restaurants nearby and soon realized he was not alone—that a growing number of non-Mexicans were doing the same. So, in 1951, Bell got into the taco business, selling tacos at his dog and burger joint for nineteen cents each. He opened and sold several taco restaurants over the next decade, then, in 1962, he opened the first Taco Bell in the Los Angeles suburb of Downey, California.

He began franchising two years later, expanding over time from California to the wide expanse of America where almost no one had ever seen a taco before. "Mexican food was really pretty unknown," says Taco Bell spokesman Matt Prince. "The experience for a lot of people was, for their first Mexican food experience, through Taco Bell. And then if you look beyond that into the sixties, his expansion was quite large, and you get into places across the country, into the middle of America, and even Florida by the end of the 1960s." Bell wrote in his autobiography, *Taco Titan*, "We changed the eating habits of an entire nation."

There are now more than seven thousand Taco Bells in more than thirty countries. A 2018 Harris poll named the chain America's favorite Mexican restaurant, even as Prince acknowledges, "Taco Bell was never in the business of replacing Mexican food, it was just taking inspiration and kind of doing its own thing." And inspiring millions of Americans to venture into not just Taco Bell, but also more culinarily ambitious Mexican American restaurants as they opened around the country.

In 2019, the upscale Mexican restaurant Cosme in New York City was ranked as the best restaurant in America—not best Mexican restaurant, but the best restaurant of any kind—on the international "Fifty Best Restaurants" list, a highly influential ranking of some of the world's most expensive places to eat. And between Taco Bell and Cosme is a huge range of Mexican or Mexican American restaurants all across the country, serving everything from the cheese-covered combination plate that Americans once saw as the pinnacle of Mexican food, to a growing variety of different foods of the many different regions of Mexico. At the same time, there is a growing point of view—which I endorse—that Mexican food and Mexican American food are two different cuisines, both deserving of respect and appreciation, but neither more legitimate than the other, with a shared history stretching back millennia.

Gustavo Arellano, author of *Taco USA: How Mexican Food Conquered America,* says, "Look at the staples of Mexican food, the beans, the corns, the chile, those started within indigenous cultures going back thousands of years." When Spanish explorers arrived in the sixteenth century, they brought their own foodways with them, which they attempted to impose after violently overthrowing the Aztec regime and seizing control of the territory they named New Spain, a vast area including more than a half-million square miles north and west of the Rio Grande river. The foods of the indigenous peoples and the conquerors would soon intermingle, with the Spanish, introducing, among other things, beef, wheat, and the technique of frying. And then those combined foodways would evolve. Differently in different places. "Mexican cuisine is better described as Mexican cuisines," says José R. Ralat, taco editor of *Texas Monthly* and author of *American Tacos: A History and Guide*, "Every region has their own signature dish and a town might have their own chili that is not found one town over. Valleys might have their own ecosystems that have micro-climates that give you different foods. So, if you want to think of French food and its highly regional cuisines, you can have a good analog here."

In 1821, a popular revolution overthrew Spanish rule and New Spain became the country of Mexico. Twenty-five years later, as a result of the Mexican American War, the United States seized half of Mexico's territory, including what would become Texas, California, and portions of New Mexico, Arizona, and Colorado. University of Texas lecturer and Director of Foodways Texas Marvin Bendele says, "When the US–Mexico War ended, they basically took hundreds of thousands of people who were Mexican citizens, and they became US citizens, albeit without the same rights as other US citizens. So, they were here and going back and forth across that new geopolitical border that was created that they'd always gone back and forth across, since it was just a river." Arellano says, "There's that saying, we didn't cross the border, the border crossed us."

And on both sides of that border, the food was the same, the food of the norteños, the residents of what had been Northern Mexico, now bisected into parts of two countries. One of many Mexican regional cuisines, it included tortillas, tamales, enchiladas, and frijoles. And it was the evolution of this cuisine—reduced in spiciness to suit Anglo tastes, and with replacements for Mexican ingredients not available here, such as American yellow cheese replacing the white cheeses of Mexico—that would form the basis of Mexican American food for two hundred years. It would combine versions of traditional dishes with others created on this side of the border. Tex-Mex combination plates, heavy on cheese and refried beans; so-called Cal-Mex dishes such as fish tacos and guacamole; green chile sauce from New Mexico; fajitas on a sizzling platter from Texas; huge Mission burritos created in San Francisco. Some combination of those and other standards became the tentpoles of a familiar Mexican American menu available pretty much anywhere.

These are definitions for many common Mexican American foods as they are most often prepared in the United States. There are many regional, local, and personal variations not reflected here.

Birria

Meat stewed in a flavorful chile-based broth, most often made with goat. An increasingly popular variety, made with beef, is called birria de res.

Burrito

A large, soft flour tortilla wrapped around various ingredients. Variations include the Mission Burrito, noted for its massive size; the California Burrito, filled with carne asada and French fries; and the Breakfast Burrito, with fillings that include scrambled eggs.

Carne Asada

Beef, marinated in citrus juices, grilled, and sliced.

Carnitas

Pork, braised or simmered with lard, crisped, and shredded.

Chili

Short for chili con carne. Originally, pieces of beef cooked with chile peppers, flavored with cumin and other spices, and sometimes tomatoes, and still frequently prepared that way in Texas, often with chili powder instead of actual chiles. Elsewhere, it is most often served as a tomato-based combination with ground beef, beans, and chili powder.

Variations include Cincinnati chili, flavored with cinnamon, and turkey chili.

Chiles Rellenos

Stuffed, battered, and deep-fried chile peppers. Cheese is the most common filling, but meat is not uncommon.

Chimichanga

A deep-fried burrito.

Enchilada

A rolled corn tortilla filled with a combination of meat, cheese, vegetables, and beans, covered with a usually chile-based sauce.

Fajitas

Marinated, grilled steak—originally skirt steak—often served on a sizzling platter and eaten with flour tortillas. Variations use other proteins, including chicken and shrimp.

Masa

Dough made from corn that has been nixtamalized, cooked in an alkaline solution usually containing lime, to make it more nutritious and usable as dough.

Mole

A sauce based on chiles, with some combination of other ingredients such as spices, nuts, fruit, and chocolate.

Quesadilla

A tortilla, topped with cheese and often other ingredients, folded over and grilled; or two tortillas, with the fillings in between, grilled and cut into wedges.

Taco

A tortilla, sometimes fried to crisp, folded over and filled with one or more proteins, cheeses, and vegetables.

Tamale

Masa, usually formed around a protein, and steamed inside a corn husk. Variations include the Hot Tamale from the Mississippi Delta, smaller, spicy, and made of cornmeal instead of masa.

Taquito

A small tortilla rolled around a filling and fried.

Tortilla

A soft, flat circle of masa or wheat flour traditionally cooked on a flat griddle called a comal.

Tostada

A deep-fried corn tortilla topped with beans and often additional ingredients.

El Indio Mexican Restaurant opened eighty years ago in San Diego. The menu has been pretty much the same for the last fifty, an assortment that includes burritos, quesadillas, enchiladas, tamales, carne asada, carnitas, and chile rellenos. "It's not fancy. It's just good food," says third-generation owner Jennifer Pesqueira, whose grandfather opened El Indio in 1940. "It's not like a five-star restaurant. But it's five-star food at prices that everybody can afford." Their signature dish is the taquito, a filled, rolled, and deep-fried tortilla. It was on their original menu and remains their signature dish today. Michelle Tomaszyk, finishing lunch with her husband and children, goes way back with El Indio. "When my mom was pregnant [with me] in 1974, she used to come to El Indio pretty much every day and get her taquitos." And the tradition continues. "I usually get the beef taquitos," she says. "And my son Jackson loves the taquitos as well."

Kathy Jahaske, here today with her daughter, who is visiting from Washington, DC, had her first El Indio taquito while sitting on the curb outside the restaurant more than forty years ago. It's been her go-to order ever since. "They're excellent," she says. "Now, I'm going toward morditidas." Those are taquitos, cut into pieces, covered with nacho cheese, then topped with sprinkles of Mexican cheese, salsa, and jalapeño slices. They were added to the menu in the mid eighties. So was the chimichanga, an Arizona favorite, when a customer came in asking for one. "Dad's never heard of a chimichanga," Pesqueira says. "This was years and years and years ago. And she described it to us, and my dad said, 'Well, yeah. We can do that. That's easy.' And basically, it's just a burrito that's deep-fried. And so, we adopted the chimichanga based on what a customer requested."

They did the same with the California Burrito. "We did add the California," she says, "because a lot of people were coming in and saying, 'I want a California' and we were like, 'What's a California?' So that's been on the menu for the last six, seven years. And that's just a burrito with French fries in it. Which to me, it still boggles my mind that people want a burrito with French fries in it."

Cassie Li does. The San Diego native now living in Denver is back visiting and that's what she ordered. "What makes this California Burrito the one that stands out would be just the way the tortilla is made," she says. "You can tell it's very fresh and then the ratio with the meat, and the fries, and the cheese, and everything's just perfect." Notice that she describes the tortilla as being "made." In most places, they're bought from a wholesaler and come out of a bag.

But at El Indio, the tortillas are made completely from scratch. This is a lengthy process. The main ingredient in tortillas is corn that has been "nixtamalized," broken down with lime—not the fruit, but the mineral of the same name—to make it edible. Most tortilla-makers buy their masa premade. El Indio makes their own. "It's time consuming, but it's a better-quality product," Pesqueira says. "It's not corn you would eat like on the cob. It's a grain, like something that cattle would eat." And breaking it down is a lengthy process. "We put it in a big tub, and we add lime," she says. "Water, of course, is the next item. And we boil it for about forty-five minutes to an hour and we let it set, soak for about twenty-four hours. The next day, we wash the corn and grind it in a big grinder. And then it becomes masa, becomes the dough. And you use that dough to make your tortillas." At El Indio, they do that on a mechanical assembly line.

This morning, Nico Robles, who has been working here since 1984, is loading big balls of masa into a feeder. They're pressed into sheets, which are cut into multiple circles of dough, then moved through a gas-fired oven on a conveyor belt three times. The tortillas emerge pillowy and flatten as they cool. At the end of the line, Alvardo Perales, who's worked here for twenty-one years, stacks them sixty to a pile, a total of about fifteen hundred tortillas by the end of day. They'll be bagged for use here at El Indio and for sale to other restaurants throughout the area. It's been done this way since Pesqueira's grandfather built his first tortilla machine by hand more than seventy-five years ago. And it's a tradition that is deeply appreciated. San Diego native and longtime customer Zabie Sahial says, "What I like most about El Indio is they make their tortillas fresh and in-house, so it's super authentic."

But how to define "authentic?" That question is at the heart of a controversy that has raged for half a century. Critics of Mexican American cooking complain that it isn't what people eat in Mexico. And largely, it isn't. As with any cuisine, Mexican food in America— or foods, given the differences between Tex-Mex, Cal-Mex and the like—have evolved over the years. Recipes have been modified. Entirely new dishes have been created, such as the massive Mission Burrito, born in San Francisco and turned into a national favorite by Chipotle. In short, over more than two centuries, Mexican American food became a cuisine of its own. Which has happened with virtually every cuisine Americans have adopted. Yet, Robb Walsh, prolific food writer and author of *The Tex Mex Cookbook: A History in Recipes and Photos*, says critics who bash Mexican American cooking don't do the same to other hybrid American cuisines: "The one example that comes to mind is Cajun food. [No one says,] 'Boy, those people don't know how to make French food. That is the most inauthentic French food I have eaten.' " Instead, the French-influenced cooking of Louisiana is embraced and respected as a highly prized cuisine of its own. This is a distinction not afforded by many to Mexican American food as it has evolved over more than two hundred years.

The assault was led by an English woman named Diana Kennedy. She moved to Mexico City when the journalist who would become her husband was stationed there for the *New York Times*. She fell in love with Mexican food, exploring the country's regional cuisines, and would become a major voice in shaping American tastes. Kennedy wrote a groundbreaking cookbook, *The Cuisines of Mexico,* published in 1972, a terrific piece of work that for the first time introduced Americans to the regional cuisines of Mexico, dishes such as cochinita pibil, Yucatan barbecued pig; budín de chícharo, pea pudding; gallina pinta, oxtail, pork, and bean soup; and pescado relleno, small red snapper stuffed with shrimp, scallop, and crabmeat.

But she did not stop with extolling the food she found in Mexico. She made it clear that she considered the American version of Mexican food a terrible bastardization of the real thing. In a later book, *The Art of Mexican Cooking*, Kennedy described how she thought Americans viewed Mexican foods: "Far too many people outside Mexico still think of them as an overly large platter of mixed messes, smothered with shrill tomato sauce, sour cream, and grated cheese preceded by a dish of mouth-searing sauce and greasy deep-fried chips. Although these do represent some of the basic foods of Mexico—in name only—they have been brought down to their lowest common denominator north of the border, on a par with the chop suey and chow mein of Chinese restaurants twenty years ago."

Kennedy's influence was immense. On the one hand, she fostered a sort of food snobbery. On the other, she opened America up to a whole new universe of Mexican food. Gustavo Arellano says, "Kennedy is important because she did care about these traditional Mexican recipes at a time where the elite in Mexico didn't. They were all about continental cuisine. Kennedy saw the greatness of these traditional dishes and traditions and went around to document them, so [she was good] in that sense. She was not good in the sense that she demonized, to this day, she'll demonize Tex-Mex food as somehow being not authentic."

Kennedy inspired a new generation of chefs to begin exploring the varieties of Mexican cuisine. Some introduced America to Mexican dishes never seen here before. Others used them as a jumping off point for new Mexican-inspired recipes. Yet others turned Mexican regional foods expensive and trendy.

But while Kennedy—and chefs she influenced—opened the door to American awareness of Mexico's varied foodways, the spread of regional dishes was truly made possible by new waves of immigration. Beginning in the seventies and eighties, many immigrants came from parts of Mexico which were not adjacent to the United States, meaning their traditional foods were not yet a part of Mexican American cuisine. Marvin Bendele says, "I think the change you actually see is those people opening up other restaurants and serving what they're used to eating." The timing was right. With the rise of the organic and farm-to-table movements, Americans were becoming more culinarily discerning and adventurous. And motivated by tastemakers such as Kennedy, many became committed to—even obsessed with—the search for "authentic" Mexican food. Even if defining that wasn't so simple.

"What's authentic to you might not be authentic to me, even though we're from the same city," says Mexico City native Claudia Alarcón, who now lives in Austin, writes frequently about Mexican food, and prefers the term "traditional" instead. "Let's talk about mole, for instance," she says. "For every person that has ever made mole, there's a different recipe, because it's one of those things where you tweak it. Your family may like more chocolate in the recipe and mine may like it spicier. Or I had my great grandmother's recipe for mole, but now I want to experiment." Many consider mole to be Mexico's national dish. Broadly speaking, it is a sauce based on chile peppers, cooked with some combination of other ingredients, which can include nuts, seeds, fruit, and chocolate. Which ones, and in what combination, are open questions, which makes the possible permutations of mole virtually incalculable.

Restaurant owner Valentin Madrid says, "Remember, in Mexico, every city, they have their own flavor, their own touch." He and his wife Rosa Hernandez came to the United States from Puebla, a city in central Mexico famed for mole poblano, roughly translated as mole from Puebla. At La Bamba, their small, plain restaurant on tourist-friendly Long Beach Island in southern New Jersey, the mole, from her mother's recipe, is extraordinary. It isn't spotlighted in any way on a menu filled with Mexican American standards. But it's there. And well worth looking for. A thick, smooth, dark brown—each taste begins chocolatey, transitions to sweet, and finishes with a substantial kick of spice. I know it well as I live on LBI, as the island is known, and La Bamba has been my go-to for years. Once a week, for several hours, Madrid says, he helps his wife make a new batch with "probably maybe around twenty, twenty-five ingredients." He's a little vague on the details, admitting only to Mexican chocolate, some kind of pepper or peppers, raisins, and bananas. "This is a big process," he says. "You have to fry each ingredient one by one. In the end, you blend." And while it wasn't a big seller at first, he says, "Maybe three, four years ago. Everything changed, the people are straight coming to eat mole."

Rosalinda Delos Santos, who lives seventy miles from LBI, in Philadelphia, says mole is quite popular there too. "Here in Philly, there's a lot of people from Puebla," she says. "My father is as well." But that isn't what she and her family are serving to customers from their silver and orange food truck in South Philly. Or any of the other Mexican dishes local residents are familiar with. "We decided to do something different," she says. "My grandma and my mom were like, 'Let's do birria, the birria tacos and see how it goes.' " Birria is a kind of stewed meat popular in central Mexico. In the state of Jalisco, it is traditionally made with goat. In neighboring Zacatecas, a version called birria de res is made with beef. On the US border in Tijuana, birria de res is popular in a taco, which is what Delos Santos's family is making from her grandmother's recipe.

"We stew the beef," she says, "marinated with like adobo with dry chilies, herbs, spices, and it's all cooked in the same pot, with the meat and everything, spices and everything, is cooked for maybe four hours, around four hours." At around six-thirty on a pleasant Sunday night in mid-December, a large pot of the cooking liquid called consommé is simmering next to a warming tray of the birria meat that had been cooked in it. They're next to the flattop grill, which Delos Santos has filled from top to bottom and side to side with double-stacked tortillas. She, her sister Brianna, and their mother Yolanda are working with both precision and speed to keep up with an unrelenting flow of orders. In other words, business as usual. "It's amazing," Delos Santos says. "We have a lot of customers. We have long lines. We open at five and there's people waiting around four." This evening, the line to order—three tacos, cheese optional, for twelve dollars—stretches all the way down the block and around the corner.

And they will sell plenty in the three hours they're open tonight. Delos Santos says, "I'm thinking probably like 250 orders." Looking at a ticket, she says, "This one right here is ten orders." That's right. Someone is going to be leaving with thirty birria tacos. But not right away. Waiting for them to be prepared can take another twenty minutes or so, as Delos Santos builds each taco step by step, entirely on the grill. She puts a serious handful of the cheese—

most are ordered that way—on top of the crisping tortillas. Then a huge portion of the meat. And a little fresh cilantro and white onion. After drenching it all with a ladleful of the consommé, which creates a cloud of aromatic steam, she flips half of the combination over, tops the now-closed taco with yet more consommé, flips the whole thing some more to make sure it's properly crisp, and then loads three of her gorgeous creations into a brown cardboard box, along with a jalapeño pepper, some pieces of onion, a slice of lime, a small container of hot sauce, and a large container of consommé for dipping the entire taco like a French dip sandwich. It's beautiful to watch and remarkable to eat. The meat, shredded and soft, but not soggy. The flavor, a remarkable combination of subtleties, bold but not too hot. Clearly worth the wait.

Dee, a nurse who didn't want to share her last name, drove forty-five minutes from Delaware to stand in line. In fact, she's the customer who's getting ten orders. She had the birria tacos once before, when her boss brought them to work for the staff. "It's delicious," she says, offering as proof, "I drove from Wilmington." She says it's worth the culinary commute. "There's no tacos like this around down there" she says. "These I love." And now, despite the drive, "I don't like any other tacos."

Bryan Kim, waiting for his order, is a first timer to this truck, which he found on Instagram, but not a first timer to birria. "I'm originally from LA," he says "So, I've just been craving some birria." In fact, California was the first place birria attracted a following beyond the Mexican American community. "The big trend in LA over the past three to four years has been birria de res tacos," says Gustavo Arellano. "I grew up eating birria de res. It was something I ate, especially at celebrations, but no restaurant would ever sell it, for whatever reason. And so, I remember when birria de res first started popping up in restaurants here in Southern California, I'm like, 'Oh, that's interesting, I wonder what's that about.' And then it blows up. I'm like, 'Oh my God, it only took you guys thirty fucking years to get with the program.' And once I saw that it spread all around Southern California, I'm like, 'Okay, this is going to be nationwide at some point.' It takes a while sometimes, but it definitely will. Then, when I saw the Pete Wells review [of a New York food truck serving birria de res tacos, published in the *New York Times* in November of 2019], I'm like, 'Oh, it's already on the Coast. Here we go.' "

To be followed by some other regional Mexican dish, as yet virtually unknown here, for Americans to "discover." Further broadening the already wide range of Mexican and Mexican American food in this country. From Mexican American classics such as smothered enchiladas and fajitas to Mexican regional dishes such as mole and birria. From fast-food drive-throughs offering Doritos tacos to fast-casual chains pouring massive frozen margaritas. From taco trucks to upscale restaurants creating remarkable food, some traditional, some invented anew, by talented chefs using heritage Mexican corn and organic ingredients. Arellano says, "The future of Mexican food is what it's always been, which is a cuisine that more and more people continue to embrace, that becomes more and more a part of the American diet."

El Indio Mashed Potato Taquitos

Recipe

Ingredients

- 4 russet potatoes (2 pounds)
- 1 green onion, finely chopped
- 3 tbsp. soft butter
- 1 tsp. chicken or vegetable broth
- ¼ tsp. garlic powder
- salt and white pepper to taste
- 1 dozen corn tortillas
- large toothpicks
- shredded jack cheese
- shredded lettuce
- diced tomato
- salsa
- sour cream (optional)
- guacamole (optional)

Directions

- Peel raw potatoes and dice them into cubes. Cover cubed potatoes with water and bring to a boil. Boil them until tender, 10 to 15 minutes. Drain out the water and mash the potatoes, while adding in soft butter, finely chopped green onion, and broth.

- Sprinkle in salt, pepper, and garlic to taste.

- Spoon some of the potato mixture into a line across a tortilla. Fold the tortilla over the potato line as the area is supported by your hand and roll it tightly. Secure it with a toothpick.

- Fry the tortilla in a pan at 350 degrees until crispy. Flip it over in oil if need be (carefully, as oil will splatter). Remove it from the oil with tongs and pat it dry with a paper towel. Let it cool before removing toothpick.

- Open the taquito flap slightly. Put salsa, cheese, and lettuce (and sour cream and guacamole if desired) on the flap opening.

Barbecue— From Shack to Chic

Brad Orrison is "on." All six-foot-two-and-a-half of him amped up in full salesman mode. Arms waving, a wide smile, a touch of red hair peeking out from under a big straw hat, he's whipping up the crowd, telling them that they are about to taste "the best barbecue out here, the most tender, luscious pork that we can make." Nonstop patter as he and a helper slam the big metal latches free with a piece of firewood and open the massive smoker built into a 1962 four-door Willys jeep, revealing two gorgeous pork shoulders, succulent and shining in the midday heat. Orrison starts ripping them into pieces by hand, the juice dripping from each ropey strand, and passing them out, with a touch of sauce, for everyone in the crowd of about thirty people to sample. Mid-bite, Johnny Newburn, who says he's been eating barbecue for sixty years, emphatically declares this batch "really good," then breaks into satisfied laughter. Kathy Mobley calls it "fantastic." Torrence Brown chooses "awesome," enthusing, "It's just tender and seasoned well and the barbecue sauce is A-OK."

This is exactly what Orrison wants to hear. Needs to hear. These tasters will be voting for their favorites in a kind of "people's choice" category here at the 2019 Memphis in May World Championship Barbecue Cooking Contest. Yes, barbecue is a big-time competitive sport now, and many consider Memphis in May to be its Super Bowl. Orrison and his team, The Shed, named for his restaurant in southern Mississippi, have won this vote several times before. But even more impressively, they've won the main event here, the overall Grand Championship, twice, most recently last year. And they're fixated on going back-to-back. "Obsessed, totally," he says. "We're all friends on Friday but come Saturday, everybody's at each other's throats. You can just feel the grit of every single team wanting and vying to be the best. It's what we live for."

It's brutal competition. And there's plenty of it. 4,500 competitors on 226 teams and 80,000 spectators filling the mile-long Tom Lee Park along the eastern bank of the Mississippi River, amid stifling heat, humidity, and the smell of barbecue smoke and rendering fat. It's a sea of white catering tents, some of them massive, multi-floored structures, almost all of them offering fresh barbecue to anyone who stops by, in direct violation of the rules. Technically, competitors don't have the licenses necessary to feed the public. The organizers make a big point of announcing that. And then forgetting about it.

In reality, this is an orgy of barbecue gluttony, of sauce and pig fat dripping down cheeks and chins. Lines of visitors shoveling from plates filled with steaming pulled pork, gnawing at ribs with the perfect pull, not quite falling off the bone but tender to the chew. With sweet sauces, vinegar sauces, and hot sauces. Pork, beef, lamb, turkey, goat, shrimp, and more, all infused with the aroma and flavor only true barbecue can provide. Phyllis Brunke, from Jackson, Missouri, who's been a judge here for twenty-six straight years, says, "When you first get here and you smell that smoke in the air, it just, oh my God, makes you weak in the knees."

For good reason. Barbecue done right—or even almost right—is a remarkable thing. And a confusing one. Traditionally, barbecue has been defined as slow, low-temperature cooking over indirect heat from hardwood coals. But as with every rule, there are exceptions, many made by some of the most respected and acclaimed pitmasters in history. Ribs grilled over direct heat at the Rendezvous in Memphis. Whole hog cooked fast and hot by legendary pitmaster Ed Mitchell in North Carolina. Pitmasters using charcoal. Even propane. In the end, defining barbecue is akin to what Supreme Court Justice Potter Stuart wrote about defining pornography: "I know it when I see it."

Memphis in May competitor David Brown from Atlanta says, "You can have all kind of flavors and seasonings and whatnot, but to get that really moist, juicy, tasty barbecue it's the technique and what you're doing and how you're doing it." High heat or low. Fast cook or slow. Wood or charcoal or even propane. When to add coals. Or rearrange them. Open pit or covered. What rub, if any, or basting sauce. Other secrets, and on and on. Techniques passed down by pitmasters from generation to generation.

The team from Big Bob Gibson Bar-B-Q in Decatur, Alabama, has won the Grand Championship at Memphis in May five times. Owner Chris Lilly, who married Big Bob's granddaughter and is the fourth generation of family to run the place, with his kids now on the job as the fifth, says, "The main thing, and what I've stressed to my children is, you don't want to screw anything up. You want to come in here and learn, because even before I got here, Big Bob Gibson had been in business for seventy-plus years or so. That's a lot of barbecue knowledge." This knowledge is considered priceless in the barbecue community, a tight club with rules, expectations, and a deep sense of history. Trimming pork shoulders in his team's tent, Tamijo Shimojo, chairman of the Japan Barbecue Association explains, "I respect American barbecue culture."

To Brad Orrison, it's a culture built on tradition. He and his sister, Brooke Orrison Lewis, who is missing Memphis in May for the first time because she just had a baby, run their Ocean Springs, Mississippi, restaurant, The Shed, together. It's an intentionally ramshackle, open-air structure with a corrugated tin roof, walls festooned with what appear to be junk sale castoffs, and strings of lights hanging from beams and crisscrossing the dining area.

The Shed offers a wide range of barbecue, from chicken, to ribs, to brisket, sausage, and more. The food is tender and juicy, served with a sauce that is bright on the tongue, spicy and sweet at the same time, clearly present but without overpowering the meat. Orrison says, "We're an old-school, low-and-slow barbecue joint that sells out of food. They always say, 'Never trust a barbecue joint that doesn't sell out of something.' "

And barbecue has been selling out all over the country, enjoying a booming renaissance after nearly disappearing from America's consciousness in the seventies and eighties. There are more than fifteen-thousand barbecue restaurants nationwide, and until the COVID-19 pandemic impacted the entire restaurant business, more were opening every day. Glowing reviews from influential food writers created long lines at the newest "discoveries" and celebrity status for their pitmasters, some of whom have even won James Beard "Best Chef" awards, considered the "Oscars of food." The Shed's pitmaster, Hobson Cherry, who'll proudly tell you he grew up in B.B. King's hometown, explains it this way: "It is the one true great American food. We adopted it to be ours and we make it in a way that nobody else in the world makes it."

The adoption papers were filed in the sixteenth century, when Spanish explorers came across the Taino people of the Caribbean. The Taino would cook reptiles, small animals, and fish over coals on a contraption made of green wood—four sticks set in the ground with a rack on top to hold the food. Mimicking the Taino word for the structure—many variations have been offered, none definitive—the Spaniards called it a barbacoa. Other explorers and settlers, finding similar methods of cooking used by natives on the American continent, transformed the Spanish word into an English approximation. Hence, barbecue. It was embraced first by settlers in the American South.

For more than two hundred years, the word "barbecue" meant an event, a large gathering, anything from holiday celebrations to political rallies, at which massive amounts of food would be cooked over coals for large crowds. Staging one was exhausting, dirty work, as Michael Twitty knows firsthand. An African American culinary historian, he has reenacted Antebellum era barbecues as teaching events, wearing period clothing, digging the pits, shoveling the coals, replenishing the wood, turning and basting the carcasses. "One of the worst things you can do in the South is cook in an open field," he says. "It's like, damn, the sun's hitting you from the top, the fire's hitting you from the bottom, it's just too much."

So, of course, it was generally African American slaves who were doing the work. And not just the physical part. It was also the slaves who created the original recipes, combining Caribbean, Native American, and African techniques and flavorings, to slowly cook an entire animal—at first whatever was available, but by the early eighteen hundreds almost always a hog—over hot coals, while basting it with some combination of spices and vinegar. Over the decades, barbecue would spread throughout the country, carried north and west in many cases as six million African Americans fled the South during the Great Migration between 1916 and 1970.

Distinct regional styles developed. Some were based on availability of ingredients, such as using beef, not pork, in Central Texas. Others reflected local tastes—German Americans are credited with the tangy sauces of the Carolinas, which are reminiscent of popular dishes in Germany, such as sauerbraten, a vinegar-marinated pot roast. John T. Edge, Director of the Southern Foodways Alliance and a prolific author on Southern food and culture says, "These styles in the beginning were, to my mind, the work of an individual pitmaster," who was then copied by enough others to create a regional standard.

KANSAS CITY

Meat:
BEEF, PORK,
CHICKEN,
TURKEY, HAM.

Signature:
BEEF BRISKET
BURNT ENDS.

Sauce:
SWEET, THICK,
TOMATO BASED.

MEMPHIS

Meat:
PORK.

Signature:
RIBS AND PULLED PORK
SANDWICHES.

Sauce:
SWEET, TOMATO BASED,
WITH MOLASSES.

Dry Rub:
SALT, PEPPER, PAPRIKA,
CAYENNE, AND SUGAR.

ALABAMA

GENERAL

Meat:
PORK.

Signature:
SHOULDERS
AND BUTTS,
PULLED.

Sauce:
SPICY,
TOMATO BASED.

NORTH

Meat:
PORK AND
CHICKEN.

Signature:
CHICKEN WITH
WHITE SAUCE.

Sauce:
MAYONNAISE
AND
VINEGAR-BASED.

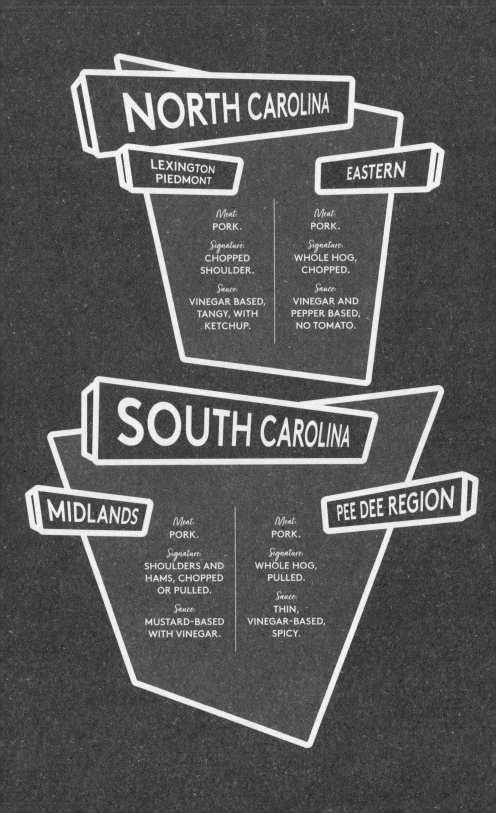

NORTH CAROLINA

LEXINGTON PIEDMONT

Meat:
PORK.

Signature:
CHOPPED
SHOULDER.

Sauce:
VINEGAR BASED,
TANGY, WITH
KETCHUP.

EASTERN

Meat:
PORK.

Signature:
WHOLE HOG,
CHOPPED.

Sauce:
VINEGAR AND
PEPPER BASED,
NO TOMATO.

SOUTH CAROLINA

MIDLANDS

Meat:
PORK.

Signature:
SHOULDERS AND
HAMS, CHOPPED
OR PULLED.

Sauce:
MUSTARD-BASED
WITH VINEGAR.

PEE DEE REGION

Meat:
PORK.

Signature:
WHOLE HOG,
PULLED.

Sauce:
THIN,
VINEGAR-BASED,
SPICY.

WESTERN

KENTUCKY

Meat:
MUTTON.

Signature:
SLICED OR PULLED.

Sauce:
WORCESTERSHIRE-BASED.

EASTERN

Meat:
PORK.

Signature:
THIN SLICED
SHOULDER, OFTEN
ON WHITE BREAD.

Sauce:
PEPPER AND
VINEGAR.

EAST

Meat:
BEEF AND PORK.

Signature:
CHOPPED SANDWICHES.

Sauce:
SWEET, THICK, TOMATO-BASED.

CENTRAL

Meat:
BEEF AND PORK.

Signature:
BEEF BRISKET, SAUSAGE.

Sauce:
THIN, TOMATO, AND VINEGAR.
FREQUENTLY OMITTED.

Dry Rub:
SALT AND PEPPER.

TEXAS

WEST (COWBOY STYLE)

Meat:
WIDE VARIETY.

Signature:
COOKING OVER DIRECT HEAT.

SOUTH

Meat:
BEEF.

Signature:
CABEZA (COW'S HEAD).

Sauce:
SWEET, MOLASSES-BASED.

By the 1920s and 1930s, barbecue had moved inside. "Barbecue restaurants really changed very much what barbecue was," says barbecue historian Robert F. Moss. "For instance, it took it from being a whole animal cooking tradition to being something where you would cook pork shoulder or ribs or brisket." There simply wasn't room in a downtown restaurant to handle a whole hog. And Moss says, "The 1940s to the 1960s, I would say, were the golden years of barbecue restaurants, where barbecue restaurants were opening just left and right. That was where you went for quick meals. Every highway was lined with barbecue stands, even fine dining restaurants were putting in barbecue pits." Until burger chains arrived, America's eating habits changed, and many pitmasters could no longer make a go of it. "A lot of those restaurants disappeared," says Moss. "The ones that have survived, those are the ones we think of as classics today."

A classic in Ayden, North Carolina, Skylight Inn BBQ, opened in 1947. Third-generation owner Sam Jones is still cooking whole hogs over wood and seasoning them with cider vinegar, salt, and hot sauce. He says, "Not cutting corners is the secret. Which is what most places fall victim to over time." And he is deeply protective of the restaurant's past. "The Skylight is one of those places, it's not to be fornicated with," Jones says. "It's an original, it's a diamond that is not to be replicated."

A classic in rural Marianna, Arkansas, Jones Bar-B-Q Diner—no relation to the Skyway's Jones family—opened around 1910 and is quite likely the oldest African American-owned restaurant in the South. Chopped pork is the only item on the menu, by the pound, or as a sandwich on Wonder Bread. Fourth-generation owner James H. Jones says it has to be Wonder Bread. "That's what my granddaddy used," he says. "It worked for them and it works for us."

A classic in the small Central Texas town of Taylor, Louie Mueller Barbecue has been run by the Mueller family since its founding in 1949. First by Louie, who began the practice of flying the American flag to let people know the restaurant is open, then his son, Bobby, then Bobby's son, Wayne, who says, "It's not an easy job, which I think is why it is so fulfilling at times. It challenges me. And it meant so much to the people before me."

His restaurant having survived all these years, Mueller now finds himself the beneficiary of changing times. "It was probably the late nineties, early two-thousands when outside-of-local-area traffic eclipsed local-area traffic," he says. Barbecue's fortunes had turned, and the country was now in the midst of a barbecue renaissance that continues today. It actually began germinating as far back as the seventies, with what John T. Edge calls "cultural spelunking." He says, "At a moment when many Americans think of the country as turning into one big strip-mall, Americans went looking for something singular and something hyper-regional and barbecue fit that bill."

Today, Mueller says, 95 percent of his clientele is from out of town. And visitors are gloriously rewarded for making the trip. Walking in through the saloon-style, swinging screen doors, it feels as if nothing at Louie Mueller's has ever changed. It's a tall and hushed space, a former school gymnasium, with shafts of diffuse light passing through windows stained by decades of smoke and grease. The signature briskets are still seasoned with a thick crust of black pepper and salt, nothing else, yet their flavor is remarkably complex. As each incredibly tender and juicy order is being sliced to be served on butcher paper, the waiting customer is given a small sample to taste. The massive beef ribs and spicy homemade sausages, exploding with juice at first bite, are phenomenal. All this is well worth lining up for.

But massive popularity does have a downside. "Most people in Taylor still only have thirty minutes for lunch," Mueller says, "and when our line is fifty people long, you can't get through." He doesn't begrudge his own success, but he does want the locals back. So, he is opening a quick service counter to sell barbecue sandwiches and tacos for ten dollars or less. The $21.50 per pound that he charges for brisket no longer makes for a cheap lunch. A few years back, he felt compelled to upscale from choice beef to more expensive prime, as did many other pitmasters. Because the rules of the game had been upended by a newcomer just down the road.

It was 2009 when Aaron Franklin opened Franklin Barbecue in an aqua and white trailer parked behind a coffee shop on the frontage road by I-35 in Austin, a couple of miles from the Texas State Capitol. His parents had briefly run a barbecue restaurant in Bryan, Texas, and he had worked for Bobby Mueller's other son, John, who had a restaurant of his own in Austin. But in barbecue circles, Franklin was a complete unknown, just thirty-one, with sideburns and Buddy Holly glasses. Traditionally, for him to become a respected pitmaster would take years. Instead, within months, Aaron Franklin was a sensation, his brisket declared by some of the barbecue cognoscenti to be the best in the country.

He took classic barbecue to a whole new level, used expensive, naturally raised prime beef, cooked over wood, and watched closely for a full eighteen hours instead of ten or twelve or fourteen, the meat and the coals being adjusted as needed, with the deepest attention to detail, in pits Franklin had modified or built himself. Franklin cut no corners whatsoever to create ribs, sausage, and especially his signature brisket, with innovations such as a sauce made with espresso. "It's a living project," he said. "It's like a hot rod that you'll never finish. It's just, we'll never get as good as we want because my expectations are so unrealistic, but it's kind of the quest. It's like 'how can I make this better?' "

Franklin had created a whole new genre of craft barbecue now being imitated all across the country. Texas barbecue historian Robb Walsh says, "Franklin is the one who really brought it to the public consciousness. I mean, he slaps that thing down, and it just wobbles, and he cuts you off a slice of it and, my God, it outclasses, the best steak you ever had. It's just amazing."

Franklin's success is legendary. Every day, hundreds of people would line up outside his building—he moved from the trailer in 2009—many with lawn chairs and beers, to wait two or three hours or more, hoping desperately that the day's supply of barbecue doesn't run out before they reach the counter. Franklin has sold out every day since opening. The only customer ever allowed to cut the line was President Obama while he was in office (he did pick up the tab for everyone behind him). When Kanye West tried to move to the front, he was refused. "The pressure is immeasurable," Franklin said. "I'll look out the window and see the line down the parking lot, starting to go up the street. You know those people are going to wait three hours. You can't serve them crappy or even something below, well, it's got to be the best thing ever." The COVID pandemic forced Franklin to change the system, allowing customers to book specific pickup times and have the barbecue brought to their cars. Barbecue that is as remarkable as ever.

In 2015, the James Beard Awards named Franklin "Best Chef Southwest," making him the first pitmaster so honored in competition with some of the country's best high-end chefs. Other barbecue restaurants had won the James Beard American Classic award, which is about Americana as much as cooking, recognizing restaurants "distinguished by their timeless appeal," serving "quality food that reflects the character of their communities," but Franklin was the first to be honored as a chef.

Daniel Vaughn, the highly influential barbecue editor of Texas Monthly Magazine says, "For me, Franklin Barbecue is in a category of its own. There is no other barbecue joint like it. And I think it created a new model for what barbecue joints could do and what barbecue joints aspire to after Franklin opened." Once Franklin rewrote the rules, a host of pitmasters and would-be pitmasters followed. Some with a background in barbecue. Some trained chefs. Some absolute newcomers. All trying to make a splash. "A lot of other barbecue joints have used them as a model but have gone much, much further in the, I guess, hoity-toity level," Vaughn says. "Some places [are] now even making their own white bread, making their own pickles."

John Shelton Reed calls it "haute barbecue." He says, "That's where you get people who are not embarrassed to call themselves chefs. Some of them are traditionalists, they're fundamentalists, who take the local barbecue style, or somebody else's barbecue style, and attempt to do it exactly right, perfect it. Then there's the ones where you have, as I say, chefs, who start cooking barbecue but they're putting their own spin on it. Sometimes, they just cut loose from any identifiable tradition at all. They're cooking different cuts of meat, they're doing it with good results, they're using interesting sauces and putting coffee grounds in it and blueberry and whatnot. And usually, they've got side dishes and desserts that are cheffy."

David Sandusky, big, bald, tattooed, with a scraggly beard, who pivoted from fine dining to barbecue in 2007 at Beast Craft BBQ Co. in Belleville, Illinois, near Saint Louis, sells wagyu beef brisket for forty dollars a pound.

At Mabel's BBQ, celebrity chef Michael Symon is making what he calls "Cleveland Barbecue," trying to create a barbecue tradition for a city that has none, by using local fruitwood and Cleveland favorites like kielbasa, Eastern European spices, and a local mustard in the sauce.

At Iron Grate Barbecue Co. in Milwaukee, classically trained chef Aaron Patin is butchering heritage hogs in-house and serving something he calls a Milwaukee rib, a rib still attached to a section of pork belly. Patin says Aaron Franklin was not his influence; he's just always done things differently.

Chris Lilly of Big Bob Gibson Bar-B-Q says, "Whether it be the finest white tablecloth in New York City or roadside diner in California, I'm seeing smoked and barbecue elements on their menu. And a lot of times, it's not traditional. Maybe it's Korean barbecue or something like that. But there's a lot of Southern barbecue techniques that are being used all over the country, all over the world, with totally different flavor profiles. And I think it's absolutely wonderful."

As barbecue became hip, self-professed foodies began debating the relative talents of pitmasters who were suddenly media stars, glowingly profiled in newspapers, magazines, and online. And while their styles and techniques may vary, almost all of these new barbecue poster children have one thing in common. They are white. This situation has increasingly come in for criticism from barbecue writers and many African American—and white— pitmasters.

John T. Edge says, "That's a problem that the white media made. And it's a problem, I think, even more so, that the competition circuit made." The competition circuit, an expensive hobby, is mostly white. It is one of the places "hip" barbecue writers find their next stars. Another is new "haute barbecue" restaurants, usually opened by young white men with financing that is harder for many African American pitmasters to obtain. In addition, fewer African American pitmasters have exploited social media and online public relations, which play a large part in getting a restaurant noticed and written about. And there is another significant factor: many African Americans working in barbecue have seen it as a dirty, low pay, low-status job they had to endure and did not want for their children.

A notable exception is an African American pitmaster raised in the business, now quite successfully out on his own and receiving glowing media coverage, Rodney Scott. A gregarious, solidly built forty-seven-year-old, burn scars on his arm attest to his chosen vocation. Scott has followed in his parents' footsteps. Rosie Scott and his wife, Ella, opened Scott's Variety, a ramshackle, tin-roofed market and gas station in Hemingway, South Carolina, shortly after Scott was born, then started cooking whole hog barbecue over coals from trees Rosie Scott himself cut down. Their son cooked his first hog at the age of eleven, eventually taking over as pitmaster in his twenties.

He explained, "We did whole hog barbecue sandwiches like most gas stations do hot dogs. It was just an extra income. Just a quick side meal. And we did it on Thursdays. And the demand of people wanting barbecue, and getting one sandwich, two, or they would buy a pound, that increased, and we went from Thursdays to Fridays. Then we moved to Saturdays, and we noticed an increase in demand, and we stopped focusing on the general store and we focused on the barbecue itself." To this day, Scott's Bar-B-Que remains one of the best reviewed barbecue spots in the country. And it remains a family operation, with Rodney Scott's parents still running the place and his son, Dominic, now tending the pits. But Rodney is no longer there.

In 2016, he struck out on his own to open Rodney Scott's Whole Hog BBQ eighty miles south of Hemingway in Charleston, South Carolina, which despite being one of the country's most vibrant food cities, had never really been known for barbecue. He began doing there what he had done in Hemingway: whole hog the old-fashioned way. "My cooking process takes about twelve hours," he said. "You're going to cook with hot coals just nice and slow, all night long."

That means burning hardwood logs in metal barrels until they are reduced to incredibly hot coals, carefully arranging those coals under a butterflied hog, and rearranging them as needed to perfectly cook the thickest portions without burning the more delicate meat. Near the end of the twelve hours, the hogs are flipped, seasoned, mopped with a vinegar and red pepper sauce, and then the various cuts and crisp skin are chopped and mixed together to achieve the perfect combination of flavors and textures. Many believe that no one does it better.

Scott's ribs, an item he never cooked in Hemingway, are just as popular. And he's branched out too, offering a smoked ribeye steak sandwich topped with cheese and onions (think cheesesteak—Scott was born in Philadelphia and the family moved to South Carolina when he was one) as well as a fried catfish sandwich. And he also serves a remarkable banana pudding made from his mother's recipe.

In 2018, just two years after Rodney Scott's opened, he won the James Beard Award for "Best Chef Southeast." To him, it's a reminder to keep doing the work. "No shortcuts," he explained on a podcast. "None. So be patient. Follow the process. Don't be in it just for fame or fortune." He added, "The week after I got back from Chicago from the [James Beard] awards ceremony, I was dumping trash and a young lady showed up and said, 'Wow. You dump your own trash.' And I said, 'Yes, why not?' "

Since then, he's expanded with his business partner from the Charleston restaurant, barbecue entrepreneur Nick Pihakis, opening a second location in Birmingham with a third planned for Atlanta, cities with no tradition of whole hog barbecue. In fact, the silos of regional style have been breached throughout barbecue country and beyond. Brisket is increasingly on the menu in the Carolinas, pulled pork in Central Texas, and sauces from every region on the same table as pitmasters give the public what it wants, pretty much every kind of barbecue they've sampled somewhere or seen on television.

Chris Lilly of Big Bob Gibson Bar-B-Q says he's been astonished by the number of restaurants now serving the unique mayonnaise and vinegar sauce Big Bob Gibson himself invented back in 1925, which became a unique component of barbecue in northern Alabama. "I'm seeing the white sauce in New York City," he says. "I'm seeing it in Napa Valley, California. I've seen it on menus in Alaska, in Miami, really all over the place, all over the world. And it's really cool to think that it started in the backyard at Big Bob Gibson's house."

When Barry Sorkin realized in his thirties that he didn't want to spend the rest of his life as a corporate IT manager, he decided to open a barbecue joint in his hometown, Chicago. But what kind? "There's so many arguments about barbecue," he says. "And I hear a lot of people talking about 'this is barbecue, and this isn't barbecue, in Texas it's this and then North Carolina's this,' and I just don't care. It's all good, you know. And I like it all."

So, Sorkin and his partners decided the menu at their restaurant, Smoque BBQ, would feature favorites from multiple regions. And he did his research. "I went down to Austin and then I ate barbecue in eighteen places in three days," he says. "I went to Kansas City and I think I did fifteen, so I did those kind of trips, but it was less to learn how to do it and more to just get a real understanding of the styles. You can't go to one place in Memphis and think you know what Memphis-style is. You have to try it all, and then you understand the range of things that is encompassed in Memphis-style barbecue."

And then he went to work, figuring out each dish by trial and error. Not exact copies of what he'd tasted elsewhere, but his take on them. "I wanted to take all those things that I liked," he says, "and make them into something that was mine. I think what makes barbecue special is that every version of it is different; it reflects what that cook had in mind." When Smoque opened in 2006, it quickly became a sensation with several food writers calling it the best barbecue in Chicago.

Smoque wasn't the first place to mix-and-match styles, but it caught the wave—now a tsunami—relatively early. Barbecue menus all over the country are increasingly mix-n-match. And "a little from everywhere" is the standard style for most barbecue chains, such as Dickey's and Famous Dave's. John Shelton Reed has dubbed any restaurant offering multiple styles, "The International House of Barbecue."

Some pitmasters and barbecue lovers are fine with the idea. Others, not so much. But most think it's here to stay. Chris Lilly says, "I absolutely don't have any problem with that. I think it's inevitable. I think there's some restaurants out there that do it really well. But I think there's some restaurants out there that totally miss the boat." Sam Jones of Skylight Inn says, "For every joint that's out there trying to do a good job, there's a dozen doing a shitty job. And because it's so trendy, a lot of people are able to get away with half-assing it."

To barbecue legend Mike Mills, the trend was understandable. "You've still got to go with what the people want," he said. "And if you listen to them when they're talking, you'll find out what they do like and what they don't like. What I do is my dad's original barbecue. And then I vary it off of that as far as flavor profile goes." Which means beef and pork on the same menu and a variety of sauces. And Mills knew how to make the kind of barbecue people hunger for. I just didn't realize it when we first met at Memphis in May, a year and a half before he would pass away.

What I saw was a seventy-nine-year-old man in jeans and a work shirt, sitting by himself at a high-top table in a mostly deserted tent. I came in to ask him a few questions because the sign out front listed his team, 17th Street Apple City BBQ, as being from Murphysboro, Illinois, and that didn't seem like championship barbecue country to me. Yes, the fellow said, he has a restaurant. Yes, he's been making barbecue since he first learned from his daddy. Only after we chatted and I went to Google did I realize who I'd been talking to, the first man ever to lead a team to three

Grand Championships at Memphis in May. He was the leader of the first team ever to receive a perfect score here, memorialized by the Memphis Commercial Appeal newspaper with the headline, "Yanks reign supreme in South's backyard," though Illinois is a long state and Murphysboro is actually farther south than Louisville.

I realized I'd actually read his book and felt like I'd interviewed Babe Ruth as if he were a rookie. When I sheepishly return to his tent the next morning, Mills shrugs it off. And then, we talk about his life in barbecue. How it had been an economical way for his family to keep good food on the table. How, as a teen, he would shoot wild game at the edge of town and bring it to the local African American barbecue joint to sell or barter for a meal. And how he helped restaurant impresario Danny Meyer open Blue Smoke, one of the country's first pan-regional barbecue restaurants, in New York City, back in 2000.

"I taught everybody there how to make barbecue," he says. "And some of the barbecue that they wanted was a learning lesson for myself because I didn't do that type of barbecue at that point in time. They were excellent chefs in their own right, but barbecue was just a stranger to them." In the end, it all comes down to fire, smoke, meat, and technique. Especially technique. As Mills tells me with a laugh, "There's a whole lot more thought put into barbecue than what most people ever dream or think that there is."

A three-minute walk from Mills's tent is The Shed's compound, a collection of tents, trailers, and an expanse of Astroturf overlooking the Mississippi River where, on the final day of competition, the team's technique is being put to the ultimate test. Today is the championship round, their whole hog to be judged against thirty-four others. They'll have to come in first, second, or third in Whole

Hog to compete for the Grand Championship against the top three in each of the two other main categories, Ribs and Shoulder. Sort of like "best in show" among different breeds in a dog show.

It's mid-morning when Brad Orrison and pitmaster Hobson Cherry open the smoker, engulfed by swirling smoke and intense heat, to inspect their hog, 290 pounds when they started cooking it twenty hours ago, and a second hog, the backup. Both look like ceramic statues, shiny, a deep tan color like a well-worn baseball mitt, and seemingly standing up, held in that position by a contraption Orrison invented called the Robo Hog (almost everyone else butterflies a whole hog, cooks it on its back, then flips it).

Orrison is keeping a smile on his face, but on this final day of competition, he is noticeably tense. So is everyone. It's in the air. Until now, the team's been competing in the so-called ancillary categories, the ones that don't count toward the Grand Championship. Today is different; everything is on the line as he and Cherry slice into the hog and begin pulling out steaming and dripping pieces from different sections. Other team members soon take over, bringing tray after tray to the prep trailer and topping the meat with sauce.

There, Orrison sifts through each tray, selects his favorite pieces, towels them off, and then squeezes some like a sponge, sometimes repeating the whole process on the same piece to get just the right proportions of meat to sauce. It is painstaking and in a stiflingly hot trailer. He calls out to no one in particular, "Could you grab us a beer?" as he fills a Styrofoam container, one piece at a time, from left to right. This is the blind-box. After it is turned in, the judges who taste the contents won't know The Shed team cooked it. All they'll see is a reference number.

As a team member takes it to the judges' tent amid cheers from the crew, Orrison's mother, Linda, says nervously, "Unless we get like a nine-eight or above, we're done." He answers, "No, we're going to get an eleven." *Spinal Tap* references aside, at this level of competition, every tenth of a point is critical. And not just from the blind-box. Those results will be combined with the scores of three judges who visit each team and do their tasting on-site.

The first arrives just a few minutes later, a stocky guy, fortyish, in a peach-colored shirt. Orrison begins ripping meat straight off the hog for him. And talking nonstop. About The Shed, the hog, and of course, the way they cooked it, not stopping as he grabs a whole hunk from the rear quarter, then a long strand of belly, holding it high in the air before handing it over. But as animated as Orrison gets, as hard as he sells, this judge is impassive, giving nothing back. No poker tell. As Orrison would say later, "Man, I was like, 'Oh, this is going to be like sandpaper.' " Still, he is trying to convince himself and his team that the visit had gone well: "I feel like it's going to be hard for him as a judge to find something that's going to beat that."

Next to arrive was a fortyish woman with her hair in a topknot, horn rimmed glasses with an ornamental chain, wearing an off-white vegetable-print blouse. And much more animated than her predecessor. As Orrison rips off a hunk of meat and begins to put it into an aluminum tray, she grabs it from him, eager for a taste. Several bites later, when he hands her a huge strip of pork belly, she says, "Oh, no. I can't eat all that." Then, she digs right in. She's an eager consumer, determined to pack away as much as she can before her fifteen minutes are over. Orrison is much happier with this round, especially with what she tells him as she leaves: "Don't throw this away, I'll be back."

She's followed by a fiftyish, relatively thin fellow with a silver mustache who is wearing a pink T-shirt and a black baseball cap. He and Orrison seem to be getting on famously, piece after piece. Orrison is chortling as he rips off a small hunk of ham and hands it over, not even bothering with the plate. He strips out a huge piece of pork belly, takes off a portion, and the judge bites right in. Then they're laughing as the judge reaches down to get yet another piece. With about a minute left in the fifteen-minute judging window, Orrison's still ripping the hog apart for him. When time runs out, the two men hug, then the judge says something and heads out. Orrison excitedly reports back to his mother, "He said, 'I can tell you this, this is the best thing I've seen today.' " Hobson Cherry adds, "And best thing I've eaten."

Cherry, who was the pitmaster for The Shed's three previous Whole Hog Championships and two World Championships, says, "We put out a great product today and I don't think we can get any better than what we got." Stealing leftovers from the prep trailer, I could not help but agree. This was, without a doubt, the finest pork I had ever eaten. Orrison was feeling good, very good, pumping his fist and telling his team to "drink beer and celebrate while we wait."

So they do, cracking beers and taking a team picture. But increasingly, the waiting begins to grate on them. It's taking far longer than in past years, or it feels that way. Then, a bombshell. The first judge, the one whose reaction had been flat, stops by to say that some of what he had sampled was imperfect, complaining that it was too moist. The team is stunned. It's the one complaint no one has ever heard before. Too dry? Sure, that would be a disaster. But too moist? Moist is the goal. It's like complaining that George Clooney and Halle Berry are just too good looking for the movies. Orrison is clearly frustrated. "The hardest thing is to keep the loin juicy or moist," he would tell me later. "And that's where he said it was too moist. The hardest thing to keep moist he said was too moist."

It wasn't a total disaster. He'd still given them a nine-point-nine out of ten. But at this level, perfection is a must, and the team is clearly rattled. What if the blind-box judges feel the same way? Or find something else to dislike? The team paces. Drinks more beer. Checks for results online. Paces again. And then, finally, the word begins filtering out. The top three finishers in Whole Hog are teams no one has ever heard of. None of the usual suspects, the other heavyweights, the past winners who are their friendly rivals. Orrison is clearly stung but does his best to remain upbeat. "No hog final," he says. "It happens." Adding with a laugh, "Hey, that hog's pretty. We should eat it." His mother, Linda, sums up her feelings in a single word: "Shit!"

The Shed would eventually finish ninth in Whole Hog, just 4.49 points behind the first-place finisher's 1,025.94 points; second in that "people's choice" category (officially called the Kingsford Tour of Champions); and seventh in Turkey Smoke (for turkey legs wrapped in gold foil). For many teams, that's a great showing. But not for The Shed. For the record, Hometown BBQ won Whole Hog, Nutt's N Butts won Ribs, and Cool Smoke won both Shoulder and the Grand Championship.

Orrison insists, graciously but not entirely convincingly, that he isn't disappointed, even though he acknowledges taking "an ass whooping." He says, "There's not one person on the team that could come up with something that we should have or could have done better when it comes to cooking that hog. It was as close as you can get. So, our game's tight and we're going to roll out the awnings and hook up the trailer and do it again next year."

Big Bob Gibson Bar-B-Q's Legendary White Sauce

Ingredients

- 1¼ cup mayonnaise
- ¾ cup distilled white vinegar
- 1 tsp. fresh lemon juice
- 1 tbsp. coarsely ground black pepper
- 1 tsp. sugar
- 1 tsp. salt

Directions

- In a medium bowl, combine the mayonnaise, vinegar, lemon juice, pepper, sugar, and salt. Use immediately or store in an airtight container in the refrigerator for up to two weeks.

The Fried Chicken Renaissance

On August 19, 2019, Bruno Cardinali, the marketing chief of the Popeye's Louisiana Kitchen fried chicken chain, was finishing up a meeting in the company's Miami test kitchen when he got a WhatsApp message on his phone. A message that would launch a war, the Chicken Sandwich War of 2019.

A week earlier, Popeye's, known for selling traditional fried chicken, had introduced a new menu item, a fried chicken sandwich, and announced it on Twitter in an attempt to grab a share of the chicken sandwich market that was dominated by one behemoth, Chick-fil-A. The message Cardinali was now reading was a heads-up that Chick-fil-A had responded with a tweet of their own: "Bun + Chicken + Pickles = all the ❤ for the original." They seemed to be accusing Popeye's of culinary plagiarism. Both sandwiches, made with a crispy fried chicken filet, pickles, and mayo, were nearly identical, as was their price, $3.99, but to Cardinali the turn of events was shocking. "Chick-fil-A doesn't engage in any conversation with competitors," he says. "The way we saw the Chick-fil-A tweet, we understood that as a response, as a literal response to our tweet a week earlier." Which meant Chick-fil-A was publicly acknowledging Popeye's new sandwich as enough of a threat to worry about.

For Cardinali, the next step was critical: "Should we engage? Should we not engage?" He quickly gathered his team in a small, white-walled, glass-fronted meeting room. Excited, phones open, no one even bothered to sit down. "Basically, it took us, I don't know, fifteen seconds to say yes, let's engage," says Cardinali, and within minutes they were tweeting back, "Y'all okay?" It was a brilliant counterstrike, implying that the market leader was overwrought, beset by the vapors, in need of a fainting couch, shaken to the core by the new competition. Cardinali won't acknowledge that, of course, but he does say their tweet "ended up playing out exactly the way we wanted."

The back and forth ignited a national social media firestorm. Suddenly, it seemed everyone had an opinion on whose chicken sandwich was best and was taking to Twitter to share it. As the tweets bounced around the internet, millions of consumers decided they wanted, needed, could not live without a fried chicken sandwich from Popeye's. Their stores were mobbed. People who had never been to a Popeye's rushed there. Customers waited in lines for hours. For a marketer, this was a grand slam home run. "When you thought about [a] chicken sandwich before August 2019, the only thing that came to mind is Chick-fil-A," says Cardinali. "And then suddenly, there's another player. There's another option." He had created a cultural phenomenon. People had to have that sandwich. Derryl Williams, hoping to attract customers to his Dallas strip club, somehow got his hands on a hundred of them, and announced he would give one away with each ten-dollar paid admission to his club. The response? "It was funny, because it wasn't all guys," he says. "We had as many females that night that just wanted to have the chicken sandwich as we did guys, so it was like, hey, I can kill two birds with one stone."

But looming over Popeye's success was a big problem, and it was getting bigger. Many of their locations had begun running out of sandwiches. Customers who had waited in hours-long lines were being sent away empty handed. Frustration boiled over into heated confrontations, even violence. After just two weeks, with their entire supply of chicken filets exhausted—after agonizing and finding no other options—Popeye's executives pulled the plug, removing the sandwich from their menu and promising to bring it back as soon as possible. Which only made people want it more. When the sandwich returned in November, so did the frenzy. Despite even more violence—which Popeye's condemned—including a fatal stabbing when a customer was caught cutting the line, sales continued to skyrocket. For Popeye's, the attendant publicity even before the sandwich came back was estimated to be worth sixty-five million dollars.

Noted food industry analyst David Portalatin says, "The launch of that item was nothing short of transformational for Popeye's' business." And great for their competitors too. "Chicken Sandwich Wars are good for everybody that has a chicken sandwich on the menu," he says, "because we rush out and we try them all. So, whether you're McDonald's, or Wendy's, or Chick-fil-A, or Popeye's, you're loving having those chicken sandwiches on the menu." For those without one, there was a stampede to join the party.

The trade publication *Nation's Restaurant News* counted more than thirty chains introducing new fried chicken sandwiches in 2020. Not just chicken chains, but also burger chains such as Fatburger, Whataburger, BurgerFi, and Hardee's; barbecue chains such as Famous Dave's and Lucille's Smokehouse; the Bob Evans family dining chain; even The Salad House, a six-unit chain in New Jersey offering what they call "health-conscious comfort food." Now, alongside three kinds of avocado toast and salads with baby kale, quinoa, roasted butternut squash, and other similar ingredients, they sell three fried chicken sandwiches—the Crispy Mutha Clucka Sandwich, a fried chicken filet with applewood smoked bacon, breaded and fried onions, cheddar cheese, barbecue glaze, iceberg lettuce, and ranch dressing; the Sweet Heat with pepper jack cheese, onions, tomatoes, chipotle aioli, and a hot honey sauce; and the Buffalo CHX with Buffalo sauce, pepper jack, iceberg lettuce, and a hot honey sauce. Corporate partner and franchise owner Jarrod Bravo says, "All our chicken is organic, hormone-free." He acknowledges, "Obviously, it's fried. We do understand that but, you know, everybody needs a cheat day." And it isn't only chains.

At the more than sixty-year-old Prince Restaurant in Saugus, Massachusetts—with checkered tablecloths inside and a forty-five-foot replica of the leaning tower of Pisa outside—owner Steven Castraberti recently added a fried chicken sandwich to his menu of pizza and Italian American classics. "It was a knee jerk reaction to what everyone else was doing," he says. "But I wanted to do it on my level." Which means a particularly tender kind of chicken breast, coated in buttermilk and panko breadcrumbs, and served on a brioche bun. "I've been very proud of the product that we're turning out," he says. "Whenever I have something new, I know right away is it going to sell or not, and it's been successful. So I'm very happy with it."

David Portalatin says, "Chicken is the number one animal protein that we consume. It surpassed beef decades ago and that relationship is never going back the other direction. And of course, when we love chicken, people might say, 'Well, it's healthier.' And yeah, there might have been some of those motivations for that long-term shift. It might also have had to do with the fact that it's less expensive over time, but don't make any mistake that we love our chicken fried." And we have for a very long time, although the origins of fried chicken in America are murky.

Scholars do agree that fried chicken first took its place on the American table in the South, and that most of its creation and development as an American dish were the work of enslaved African Americans cooking for slaveholders. But what was the starting point? Some historians argue that fried chicken as made in America was related to some forms of chicken cooked in Africa. Others, that it had historically been cooked in Scotland, was brought to America by Scottish settlers, then increased in popularity after being included in early cookbooks. Many scholars have concluded it's probably all of the above.

Historically, fried chicken was eaten by both Blacks and Whites in the South, despite vicious racist stereotypes which grew up around the dish and have still not been completely eradicated. Adrian Miller, author of *Soul Food: The Surprising Story of an American Cuisine, One Plate at a Time,* says, "It's so immersed in Southern culture. It's part of private dinners, it's part of family reunions, church functions, and any special occasion. So, I think it just permeates both cultures." His conclusion? "I think of it as a Southern dish both claimed by African Americans and Whites."

It was also in the South that the business of selling fried chicken was born, most prominently in the late nineteenth century after the end of slavery as one of the few income sources available to African American women. Known as waiter carriers, they sold fried chicken to train passengers. The best documented waiter carriers were from Gordonsville, Virginia. According to Psyche Williams-Forson, author of *Building Houses out of Chicken Legs: Black Women, Food, and Power,* "They sold chicken and other foods at the railroad stations in Orange County and in the Gordonsville area. *Harper's Weekly* captured the enterprise and said not only was it women, but children and men as well. And that when the trains would come to the depot, these women would rush to the windows and lift their platters up and folks would make purchases."

And while the waiter carriers of Gordonsville are the best known, there were others too. Williams-Forson says, "There were many. I have a picture of a woman that was drawn who was selling chicken in Richmond at the train station. And then there are some others who conducted this enterprise down south, further down south. So, it's verifiable that it's a legitimate enterprise." It lasted, at least in Gordonsville, until the 1930s or 1940s.

It was the Great Migration—Blacks fleeing the South for Northern and Western cities—that first brought fried chicken to the rest of the country. Miller says, "They frequently called it Southern Fried Chicken. And it wasn't just African American-run restaurants. But in a lot of the white-run restaurants, you did have African American cooks at the helm." By the fifties, the word was out. "If you look at newspapers, magazines, and stuff, a lot of people were writing about Southern Fried Chicken. And you had a lot of restaurants popping up all over the country, way before Colonel Sanders, that were serving fried chicken."

But it was Kentucky Colonel Harlan Sanders—it's a purely ceremonial title—who would institutionalize this Southern dish as an American standard everywhere, from the biggest cities to the smallest towns. By 1955, after a life of successes followed by failures in various ventures, he was succeeding again, making an excellent living from a café he had opened in the small Appalachian town of Corbin, Kentucky. It was located on US Highway 25, part of a main route for travelers between the Midwest and Florida, a combination of roads known as the Dixie Highway. Those travelers had to eat somewhere, so Sanders's business was booming. Until, suddenly, it was gone. The Corbin section of new interstate highway I-75 opened, taking all of that traffic away from Sanders's café. His customers disappeared. At the age of sixty-five, he had to start over yet again.

This time, he gambled on franchising, selling other restaurateurs the right and tools to sell what had been one of the most popular dishes at his café, fried chicken. Sanders was an excellent cook, and his chicken was apparently delicious. But unlike hamburgers—quick and simple to make, thus perfect for fast food and franchising—fried chicken required a recipe, at least some cooking skill, and a substantial amount of cooking time. But Sanders figured out a way to simplify and quicken the process—dropping it to nine minutes from thirty—by replacing skillets full of grease with pressure cookers, which he sold to franchisees along with his proprietary seasoned flour, presumably containing some iteration of his now-legendary eleven herbs and spices. He also took a cut of each franchisee's revenue, initially five cents per chicken.

And it worked. From that modest beginning, Kentucky Fried Chicken would completely upend and reinvent the chicken business, spawn a host of competitors including Popeye's, Church's, and Bojangles, be sold to and by a string of huge corporations, flourish or flounder depending on who was in charge at the time, and end up today as one of the world's best-known brands with more than four-thousand locations in America, more than twenty-three-thousand outlets in more than 140 countries and territories worldwide, and with a continuing string of new competitors entering the market every year.

Still, chain chicken hasn't totally taken over. In town after town, city after city, the classics survive—restaurants, often family-owned for generations with recipes passed down from the beginning where the fried chicken is made entirely by hand and served by people who care deeply about what they're cooking.

Places like Ms. Girlee's Soul Food Restaurant, a narrow storefront among many in a block-long, tan brick building in Memphis. Inside, on this Wednesday in early December, eighty-one-year-old Jimmie Leach, known as Mama, sits in a corner booth keeping an eye on everything. She bought the business with her late husband Baxter in 1985 and still takes her turn cooking. But these days, her oldest daughter Enkia, known as Auntie Anita, manages the place, supervising seven other family members and serving many other families who've been eating here for years. Auntie Anita says, "The parents grew up coming to the restaurant and now the grandchildren come and they're all school mates with some of our grandchildren."

"Me and my family go there all the time," says Christina McCarter, who runs food tours for Memphis tourists and has been eating Ms. Girlee's fried chicken for years. "It's lightly breaded. It's not a bunch of flour," she says. "I like lightly breaded chicken, but still crunchy." The breading is flour with some half-dozen spices mixed in, garlic powder and lemon pepper the most noticeable, a big batch made every day at five in the morning. And the rest of the recipe is as basic as fried chicken can get. No brine. No buttermilk. No egg wash. Just chicken pieces breaded and dropped into oil that's as much as fifty or seventy-five degrees cooler than the three-fifty most recipes call for.

The result is remarkable. "The skin is crispy and delicious," says a first timer named Bob. "The breast meat is more flavorful than I have ever had in a fried chicken and retained a lot of moisture." Auntie Anita says it's Momma's recipe, unchanged for decades. "My mom said, 'do it with love, just do your best.' " And they are, selling twelve or thirteen-hundred pounds of fried chicken every week. Longtime customer Lisa Collins says, simply, "They know they are the best in town."

While classics such as Ms. Girlee's keep on brilliantly doing what they've always done with a loyal customer base that isn't leaving anytime soon, the fried chicken business continues to change around them. Attracting multi-Michelin-starred chefs such as Thomas Keller, who serves buttermilk fried chicken at his Ad Hoc restaurant in Yountville, California, and Grant Achatz, who offers fried chicken and waffles with honey butter and whiskey syrup at his restaurant Roister in Chicago.

And there is a growing variety of styles. "We're in a moment where fried chicken has taken so many iterations, we're looking around the world for inspiration, for flavors," says Adrian Miller. Chains from various countries are entering the American market. The Bonchon chain introducing twice-fried Korean-style chicken. Pollo Campero offering adobo-seasoned Guatemalan chicken. And there's Japanese fried chicken. Indonesian. Indian. Brazilian. And more.

But the geographical style making the biggest impact over the last few years isn't from another country; it's Nashville Hot Chicken from Tennessee, amped up with enough spice to set mouths afire and cause uncontrollable sweating and tears. Once unknown outside of Nashville, hot chicken has been spreading all across the country, restaurateurs trying to replicate the legendary fire and flavor of the chicken from such Nashville stalwarts as Hattie B's, Bolton's, Bishop's, and especially the place that started it all, Prince's Hot Chicken. "Prince's is the mother church of hot chicken," says Bill Purcell, who created the first Music City Hot Chicken Festival when he was Nashville's mayor back 2007. "I've tried most everything," he says. "But at the end of the day, Prince's did it first and Prince's does it best."

Prince's oft-repeated, generally accepted, and ultimately unprovable origin story has pig farmer Thornton Prince III, an inveterate womanizer, coming home to a seriously angry girlfriend after a very late night out. When he asked her for something to eat, she went for revenge, making him fried chicken so spicy it would be either painful or impossible to eat. Instead, the story goes, he loved it and soon started selling it, probably out of his house at first and then at the restaurant he opened in 1936.

Current owner Andre Prince, Thornton's great-niece, remembers her father bringing hot chicken home for her and her two siblings to share the next morning. "We'd be so anxious to be the first to wake up and get to it," she says. "He never brought home any more than two pieces for us to divide and argue over. But I always remember that greasy bag on the stove and I looked forward to it. It's amazing." This assessment is shared and emphatically repeated by customer after customer all these years later.

"It's the best fucking chicken in the world," says Matt Madden, eating here for the third time this week. "You can't deny it. Once you take a bite of it, you're hooked." It's an excellent example of what fried chicken should be—tasty, juicy, crispy skin. But most memorably, it brings the heat. "That first bite," says Madden, "it's just overwhelming and so powerful in your mouth that it just wakes you up."

The cause of that wakeup call is a closely guarded secret, apparently involving a fiery marinade, spiced flour, and some kind of liquid slathered over the chicken when it's done. As to specific ingredients, Prince will only say, "It's basically cayenne and that's as far as we go with that." And she won't allow visitors into the kitchen either, though a limited view from a vantage point next to the men's room does provide a glimpse—about ten people, some dredging chicken at a prep station in the middle of the room, others dropping it into deep friers along the walls. When they're done, the glistening chicken pieces are topped with a few sliced pickles and served on plain white bread, which then turns increasingly red as the chicken's juices and oil soak in to create an otherworldly combination. "The grease bread, and the chicken flavor, there's nothing like it, really," says Gary Lowe, who's been eating at Prince's since 1954.

Newlyweds Zoe Stadler and Cody Dierkes have been eating at Prince's since about an hour ago. First timers here, they've driven down from St. Louis. "My aunt and uncle, they recommended it." Cody says. "They were like, 'Go have some Prince's on us.' " So, they're having an experience unlike any they've ever had before. "My mouth was burning after the mild," Zoe says. And after a bite of the medium, "I was crying." Cody chose hot. "I couldn't go any higher than that," he says. "My mouth is still on fire. But it's a good burn."

Former Mayor Purcell, who's just polished off a hot leg, says, "People ask what they should order, and my answer is, 'It's a hot chicken restaurant. If you want a medium chicken or a mild chicken, you should go to a medium chicken restaurant or a mild chicken restaurant.' " But in reality, Purcell is welcoming of people eating hot chicken however and wherever they like it, even at Kentucky Fried Chicken, which sells its own far less spicy version of the dish all across the country. "I think imitation is the finest form of flattery," he says. "Anything can be a gateway to the real hot chicken."

Andre Prince says, "To me, it's a tribute to how good it is." This tribute has turned an obscure local dish into a celebrated national phenomenon. By established chains adding it to their menus; by new chains specializing in the dish, such as Dave's Hot Chicken, born in Los Angeles and now planning to franchise nationally with funding from an investment group that includes Maria Shriver, Samuel L. Jackson, and Michael Strahan; and by independent restaurants such as Hot Chicken Takeover, a Midwestern hot chicken pioneer opened by Joe DeLoss in his hometown of Columbus, Ohio, in 2014. He says, "My wife and I took a trip down to Nashville when we were expecting our first daughter and just kind of ate our way through the city and stumbled upon hot chicken based on the recommendation of a lot of folks and really fell in love with it."

Back home, he began trying to teach himself to recreate the experience. "We bought an eighty-dollar Bed Bath & Beyond deep fryer," he says. "And that's what I learned on." He learned it well enough to go into the hot chicken business, first opening a weekend pop-up up, then a restaurant, then several more. Today, there are five, with additional expansion planned.

"We had a pretty meteoric rise," he says. But it wasn't simple. "Because we were really the first hot chicken operator in our region, a lot of our effort was spent around educating people on the tradition of Nashville hot chicken, both its preparation and the culture of food eaters around it. And so, a lot of our early days were spent kind of convincing people that it was a good idea and that their face should be melting off." But he did eventually face reality. "Our hot chicken is dialed back on the spice level about one step from Nashville. It wasn't initially, but our Midwest eaters really needed the relief." Still, he was careful not to go too far. "First things first, hot chicken should be hot," he says. "A lot of brands have watered it down pretty significantly or really tried to leverage the food trend to appeal to the masses." Who continue to crave fried chicken in whatever form.

"The American consumer loves to try new things, especially if it's something we're already familiar with," says David Portalatin. "Among the fastest growing restaurants in America today are concepts around chicken tenders, or strips, or whatever name you want to call them by. Whether that's the fast-casual concept Raising Cane's, or Zaxby's, or some of these others." That's right, the latest big thing in chicken used to be the centerpiece of the children's menu. Raising Cane's sells nothing but chicken fingers and sides. It's now the fourth largest chicken chain in America by sales, after only Chick-fil-A, Kentucky Fried Chicken, and Popeye's. Goldman Sachs recently bought a piece of Zaxby's, which sells chicken fingers and wings, and recently added sandwiches, with the promotional slogan, "The Chicken Sandwich War ain't over yet."

Not that the big guns are getting complacent. Chick-fil-A recently tested a version of their sandwich topped with pimento cheese, honey, and jalapeños. Popeye's tested a BBQ Bacon Cheddar Chicken sandwich, presumably developed in the same kitchen where marketing chief Bruno Cardinali got the message that led to the Chicken Sandwich War in the first place. Cardinali was born in Brazil and has lived all over the world, where he learned about selling different products to different cultures. He has concluded that Americans have a historic emotional connection to fried chicken. "It's a food that brings comfort," he says. "It's a food that brings joy. It's a food that brings togetherness."

Prince Restaurant
Chicken Sandwich

Ingredients

- 4 oz. boneless, skinless chicken breast
- buttermilk for dredge
- panko breadcrumbs for dredge
- soy or vegetable oil
- 3 pickle chips
- 1 slice of tomato
- 3 leaves of lettuce
- 1 brioche roll
- topping sauce of choice

Directions

- Butterfly and gently pound the chicken. Dredge it in buttermilk and then in panko breadcrumbs. Fry the chicken in oil.

- Warm the roll. Spread both sides of the roll with sauce. Add the chicken breast. Top the sandwich with pickle chips, tomato, and lettuce.

On a Roll— The American Sushi Story

A grey Ram pickup pulls into a gas station across from Walmart at the busy intersection of South Sooner Road and Southeast Fifteenth Street in the Oklahoma City suburb of Del City. The driver's door opens, and Daniel Lee gets out. A stocky, middle-aged man with short, grey-flecked, curly brown hair, and a mostly greying, close-clipped mustache running all the way down to his chin, he fills up his truck and heads into what looks like just another combination gas station and convenience store. But this one's a little different. Beyond the rows of chips, snacks, and soft drinks, next to a big semi-circular Bud Light sign and a selection of CBD products, Lee sees a sushi chef hard at work below a red paper lantern, slicing fish and rolling it in seaweed. A full sushi bar. At a gas station. "I just noticed it," he says. "I was filling up with gas, come in to pay for it and seen it. And I like sushi, so I thought I'd give it a try." At a gas station? "Yeah. I wondered that before I did it," he says. "But, hey, I'm game, I'll try anything, yeah. And it tastes good." Of course it does, according to owner Annie Shahadat. She says, "Everything is made from scratch every morning, and because it's made fresh, it tastes completely different."

Shahadat was born in Bangladesh but has spent most of her life in Oklahoma. She and her husband took over the gas station in

2006 and added the sushi bar, which they named the Ninja Sushi Station, in 2013. "We wanted something unique to the town. Sushi was the first thing that came into my mind," she says, not that her customers had been clamoring for it at every fill-up. "People laughed at us," she says. "But when they see that we make it right front of them, they like it." And they like the price, as little as a dollar per piece. "Since it's not a dine-in place or a fancy place, we can keep it a little bit low," she says. "And if somebody wants to get themself introduced to sushi, they can try it."

And the introduction need not be culinarily intimidating. Ninja chef Nova Fadil says, "Our specialty right here is the deep-fried sushi." Perfect for new customers afraid of raw fish, he says: "They're always asking, 'is it cooked or raw?' and we always offer the deep-fried one. And they always come back for more because of that." The popularity of the deep-fried dishes is obvious, from the sizzle of the oil to the smell in the air. Fadil's deep-fried specialties include a Tiger Roll with green onion, crawfish, and tempura shrimp, and a Ninja Roll, with green onion, cream cheese, lemon, tuna, salmon, and shrimp. He also makes a fried chicken roll.

Not that everyone wants their sushi deep-fried; Johnathan Shelton, young and fit, with a neat beard surrounding an easy smile, says there's already too much fried food in the Oklahoma diet. He's here for something lighter. "We work outside a lot," he says. "Heavy food is not good. And this is, it's crazy because this fills you up. It don't drag you down." Shelton's having a Spicy Sooner roll, a brightly colored cylinder of rice and seaweed with cream cheese, imitation crab, and tempura shrimp on the inside—the tail of the shrimp actually poking out of one end—and white and orange lines of spicy mayo and wasabi mayo on the outside. And he loves it. "I don't even compare it to California. I compare this sushi to Hawaii," he says. "The way it looks, the way it feels, I feel like I'm in Hawaii or something."

While gas station sushi is still a punch line for many people, the joke has long been fading all across the country. Sushi is now available seemingly everywhere—gas stations, convenience stores, supermarkets, college campuses, hospitals, baseball stadiums—in many cases replacing traditional American fast food such as hot dogs and hamburgers. At the same time, it is featured at some of the country's most upscale restaurants. At Masa in New York, often called the most expensive restaurant in America, a sushi dinner is $595 per person.

But there are sushi bars and restaurants in every price range from coast to coast, serving gorgeous circles of sliced sushi rolls called maki, with rice and a rainbow of ingredients wrapped in a dried seaweed called nori; other rolls called uramaki, with rice on the outside of the nori, often dotted with shiny orange fish roe called tobiko; temaki, cones of dark seaweed filled with rice and fish, vegetables, or both, known as hand rolls; and nigiri, rice topped with artfully sliced fish in hues ranging from deep red to almost translucent. Sliced fish without rice, called sashimi, while not considered sushi in Japan, has nonetheless become a staple at sushi bars in America.

Samuels Seafood company provides fish to more than five hundred sushi restaurants. Shortly after six o'clock on a cold March morning, I'm in their cavernous Philadelphia facility within sight of the city's football and baseball stadiums. They'll process twenty-thousand pounds of fish here today. Vice President Joe Lasprogata escorts me to the cutting room, where there is constant activity, everyone in boots and protective smocks at as many as a dozen cutting tables. On the far side of the room, a slight man in a yellow waterproof apron is opening a long Styrofoam container and removing a massive fish, a beautiful yellowfin tuna from South Africa—silver grey, headless, gutted, and ready to break down. With a long, thin knife he cuts off the tail and the section encircling the front of the body called the collar, slices the fish all the way down its back, then down the belly, and opens it like a book to reveal a mass of gorgeous, deep red flesh, which becomes even redder as the hemoglobin in the fish interacts with the air. Lasprogata is pleased. "This is a nice tuna," he says. "There's no problem with that fish at all. It's certainly appropriate to be eaten raw." And he tells me 80 percent of all the tuna they process ends up as sushi or in some other uncooked dish like poke.

After all, the vast majority of traditional sushi contains fish. But what many, if not most people don't realize is that sushi doesn't actually require fish at all. When it's included, it need not be raw. And plenty of sushi is made with vegetables instead. In fact, Ken Woytisek, who taught Asian cuisine during twenty-one years at the Culinary Institute of America, says, "It's not about the ingredients that go into making the sushi, it's about the rice." Short grained, seasoned with rice vinegar and usually sugar and salt. "In Japan, a sushi apprentice spends two years learning how to cook rice," he says. "And they won't let them do anything else but cook the rice and prepare the rice because that's what it's all about. It's the rice. What goes into it is secondary. However, I think here in the US we tend to think about the other things, the other ingredients that go into sushi, like the fish."

And yes, sushi did begin with fish a long time ago. As far back as the twelfth century, people in Japan would preserve fish by packing it in rice and leaving it for months. The acids created as the rice decayed would keep the fish from rotting. The rice itself, described as tasting like "the vomit of a drunkard," was discarded. A couple of centuries later, however, people began eating sushi much earlier in the preservation process, and at that stage they found the rice actually tasted good and could be eaten instead of being thrown out. By the early nineteenth century, sushi had evolved into something we would recognize today—flavored rice, usually containing vinegar and often other ingredients such as sugar or salt, pressed together in the chef's hand, topped with something, usually fish, and served absolutely fresh: nigiri.

Sushi began to develop a small following in America after the Second World War amid Japan's economic rebuilding when Japanese companies were sending executives to Los Angeles. The first sushi bar there opened in 1964 and others soon followed, still serving a Japanese clientele. But then something remarkable happened— sushi became hip in Hollywood, discovered by movie and television stars, musicians, entertainment executives, and agents.

Among the very first was Yul Brynner, best known for his Tony and Oscar winning performances in the Broadway musical and Hollywood film *The King and I*. He would frequently lunch at a sushi bar called Osho next door to Twentieth Century Fox. A multitude of other celebrities was soon seen eating sushi as well. And the beautiful people. The style-setters. Tastemakers. Trendsetters. Not just in Los Angeles. Brynner's daughter Victoria says her first memory of going to a sushi bar was with her father in New York. "I remember clearly going there and he would order these huge platters of sashimi," she says. "He would order lobster and it would still be moving when it was on the plates, all cut up. And he thought that was just thrilling. He thought that was just the most exciting, fun thing ever."

And Hollywood contributed in another way as well. In 1980, Actor Richard Chamberlain starred in the NBC miniseries *Shogun*, set in early seventeenth century Japan, which generated a massive wave of popular interest in all things Japanese. Noted sushi chef, teacher, and cookbook author Hiroko Shimbo says, "*Shogun*, I think, has a huge impact on the popularization of sushi." Chamberlain himself recently told an interviewer, "We put sushi on the map."

Yet another big factor was health. A United States Senate report released in 1977 tied the American diet to disease and recommended more consumption of fish. At the same time, legendary American chef Alice Waters was promoting a new kind of lighter American cooking based on fresh, local ingredients served in a simpler way. All of these factors converged to make sushi desirable, or at least aspirational, all across the country.

Sasha Issenberg, who wrote the authoritative book *The Sushi Economy*, says, "You get the string of things like it's showing up in pop culture coverage as here's the thing that the actors eat, and it was exotic and it was new, and it suggested that this was a thing that healthy, beautiful people ate, and that it was part of a desirable lifestyle."

And for those still squeamish about raw fish, there was the California roll, created in in the late sixties or early seventies, though exactly when and by whom are hotly disputed. The California roll did away with raw fish entirely, and is usually made of avocado, cooked crab (or more frequently these days, imitation crab), cucumber, and sometimes mayonnaise, all surrounded by vinegared rice and nori seaweed. Some say it was meant to appeal to Americans. Others contend it was initially aimed at Japanese customers when fatty tuna was unavailable, substituting the texture of the avocado for the fattiness of the fish. One decision clearly made to please Americans was moving the rice from inside the seaweed to outside. Hiroko Shimbo explains, "The whole purpose of making rice outside is to make the nori disappear inside of the roll," since many Americans just didn't like biting into a piece of black seaweed.

The California roll remains one of America's favorite forms of sushi to this day. And as the game changer, America's gateway drug to sushi, it opened the door to dozens of different varieties of American sushi rolls. Many, if not most, are bigger, stuffed with more ingredients than the traditional maki roll served in Japan, and often awash in flavors. Shimbo says, "Americans love sauces, so the rolls are heavily painted or sauced on top of the maki rolls. Like Americans created pizza, not the Italian way, but the American way. It was made to appeal to an American audience."

Like a dynamite roll with yellowtail, shrimp tempura, and vegetables, with rice on the outside, topped with spicy mayonnaise, then quickly baked, grilled, or torched to cook the mayonnaise. There's the Philadelphia roll, often called the Philly roll, with smoked salmon, asparagus, avocado, and most notably cream cheese, which has never been part of the Japanese diet. The spicy tuna roll hides leftover tuna scraps under a spicy, often mayo-based sauce. The spider roll contains an entire deep-fried softshell crab. And there are dozens more. Further broadening the variety, different chefs have different recipes for rolls of the same name. And new rolls are being invented all the time, all Instagram ready.

Ken Woytisek says, "People are always looking for the new, what's new, I want to try something different. You wouldn't see things in a traditional Japanese sushi restaurant like dragon rolls or things like that. We've manipulated the recipes so much that in many cases the kind of sushi that we eat here would be unrecognizable in Japan." Though he adds, "I don't think it's a bad thing. One of my favorite rolls is the softshell crab roll, which you now find even being offered in traditional Japanese restaurants." He says sushi is now part of the American culture. "We see it as something that is almost as this is an American food because we have made it American."

Sushi chef and cookbook author Marisa Baggett says, "I absolutely think that sushi is an American food."

Baggett teaches sushi-making classes in her home kitchen in Memphis. When I asked to attend one, pre-COVID, she recruited several friends, a group of casually dressed young professionals arrayed around the smooth acacia wood counter in her spacious, open kitchen. "The point is to empower you," she tells them. "To figure out what you like the most in sushi and be able to recreate it at home."

She wants to puncture the exotic mystique around sushi, to eliminate the fear, even about ingredients. "Please, please, please, do me a favor and do not buy sushi rice that's packaged as sushi rice," she says, urging the class to buy medium or short grain California rice instead. "It's the same thing," she says, "but if they stick the word sushi on it, they know that they can charge you more."

With that same down-to-earth attitude, she guides the class through making three different kinds of sushi rolls. First, a hosomaki, a small, basic Japanese roll, this one with only cucumber and sesame seeds inside the rice and nori. And for a first attempt, the class does okay. Britany Usiak says, assessing her work, "It's falling apart, but delicious."

After completing the next one, a larger roll called a futomaki, filled with smoked salmon, avocado, and cucumber, Justin Waldrip says, "I think I'm feeling better all across the board with this." By the time they each complete their third roll, what's called a uramaki, with rice and sesame seeds on the outside and raw salmon, avocado, and cucumber on the inside, there's a palpable sense of success. Danny Kraft says, "This is some of the best sushi I've had. And I don't know if that's because it's the highest quality or because I had the experience of making it."

Brittany says, "It seems much less intimidating than it was."

Baggett, an expert highly trained in making classic Japanese sushi, makes no apology for teaching American favorites like the inside-out roll. "I'm obviously a sushi snob," she says, "but my sushi snobbery is not about the ingredients, so much as the preparation of it." Even if it isn't traditionally Japanese. "A very well-made California roll can be absolutely delicious," she says. "Traditional sushi, there's a lot less rolls involved, and in America we are definitely a roll centric sushi fan base. We like a lot of stuff in our sushi, where traditionally sushi is very simple, and has few ingredients."

Some of the most traditionally Japanese sushi can be found in places that might seem unexpected. Like Marysville, Ohio; Georgetown, Kentucky; or Smyrna, Tennessee. These communities and others, mostly in the southeast, are home to Japanese-owned auto plants and parts suppliers. And restaurants and sushi bars fighting for their Japanese employees' business. Greg Askew, Assistant Chief Engineer for Honda in North America, who is based in central Ohio and has traveled to Japan on business more than two dozen times, says, "Find the right place, you can close your eyes and you'd think you're in Japan."

Many Americans in the area have come to love that kind of sushi. For those who have not, there's always an Americanized option. Benjamin Pachter, Executive Director of the Japan-American Society of Central Ohio, says, "So many successful restaurants are able to provide both experiences. You can have a basic traditional sushi experience. Not just in terms of type of fish, but you're also going to get fish roe or eel or octopus or those sorts of elements. But you also have the rolls. The California rolls, the different types of rolls that are more of an American development."

Tokyo-born Tomoka Logan runs School Sushi—as in school of fish—in an old bank building in Lexington, Kentucky. She says many of her regular patrons are Japanese. "Most Japanese customers work for [the] automotive industry," she says. "Because we have a big Toyota plant in Kentucky, and all the other related suppliers." The plant, where her American-born husband works as an executive, is in nearby Georgetown, Kentucky. At School, she offers his Japanese counterparts a taste of home, a taste many of her American customers have also come to love. "Of course, people like the California [roll]," she says, "and probably 50 percent of American local people still like those kinds of rolls. But the other half of people seems like [they] want to try something different than a California."

"I like the raw sushi," says Sandra Li, who came to School on the spur of the moment this evening with her boyfriend Alex Dandoski He says, "We had yellow tail tuna, white tuna, and salmon, as well as the salmon avocado roll." And he adds, "If deep-fried sushi rolls are your thing, then there are some other places that deep fry a lot more sushi."

"It's super fresh," says another customer, Madeleine Kissinger. "You go to a sushi restaurant in Lexington, you pretty much know that you're going to get good sushi." And she says word around town is that Toyota requires it: "They said, 'Yeah, we will set up a factory here, but our one request is to have weekly, fresh shipments of fish.' " Which sounds like an urban legend, until the President of Toyota Kentucky, Susan Elkington, tells me that, while there was nothing in writing, it was a real consideration. "It's not like the deal point that's going to make or break the decision, but it was important that there was availability," she says, part of making sure Toyota's Japanese employees would be comfortable living in Kentucky."

This has left locals, such as self-described "sushi girls" Tricia Benavente and Andrea Clemons, ecstatic. "It was amazing, it was delicious," says Clemons of this evening's meal at School. Benavente says, "Oh my gosh, it's authentic, it's fresh." And when it comes time to order, they leave that up to the sushi chef. "He chooses the fish," Clemons says, "we always do that." "We just trust it," says Benavente, "when the plate came and I looked at it, I was like, 'Oh yeah.' "

There's actually a Japanese word for ordering that way—omakase. Tomoka Logan says, "Omakase means up to chef. Chef knows what's good, what's available, and what he wants to offer to the customer." And it's what she prefers: "I think that's the best way to go. If I'm the customer, I always do omakase." In fact, omakase has been exploding in popularity in the past few years, most notably in New York and Los Angeles. Eater critic Ryan Sutton has written that "high-end Japanese has supplanted fancy French or American as the prevailing medium for ultra-luxe and unrestrained blowout dining." It's a financial reminder of what sushi in America used to be before it became nearly ubiquitous, available everywhere from convenience stores to strip malls.

Sasha Issenberg says, "It is unusual to have an ethnic food in the United States basically migrate downward from being a taste for the elites rather than upward from immigrant enclaves. Sushi was an expensive and fancy thing in the beginning, and it's taken fifty years for it to trickle down to being the thing that you can get the cheap version of in a casual environment." Not necessarily a Japanese environment either. Restaurants serving other Asian food, such as Chinese, Korean, and Thai often also have sushi on the menu, even though it has never been a part of those cuisines.

Even basic American restaurants have found a market for sushi. When sisters Lisa Randall and Carrie Leary were looking for something to boost their business at Casagranda's Steakhouse in an old brick warehouse in Butte, Montana, they gambled on sushi night. A decade later, it remains a massive success. Randall says. "It's a night out even for people that don't necessarily do sushi." And for those who don't, there's always an inside-out roll filled with chicken strips, French fries, and "volcano sauce;" another roll filled with pickle, mustard, onion, and homemade pork chop; or the Casagranda roll, with sirloin steak, cream cheese, scallion, mild peppers, and cayenne pepper.

"Sushi has become comfort food," says Tracey Schram, Vice President of major sushi supplier Fuji Food Products. "When you look at the Millennials, this is something that's their go-to food. Where us, it would've been a burger and fries. For that generation, it's sushi." Schram's company produces prepackaged sushi. Inside their 3,500 square foot Brockton, Massachusetts, production facility, four automated production lines spit out thousands of sushi rolls each month, cut into pieces, packed into plastic trays, and trucked off to hundreds of supermarkets in the eastern part of the US. A similar plant in Santa Fe Springs, California, supplies the rest of the country. And they do it with relatively little human involvement.

"The rice is cooked and seasoned with sushi vinegar and, once that process is completed, the rice is cooled down, and then it's transferred over to what we call a sushi robot," Schram says. "The rice is fed into the hopper of the sushi robot, and it comes out onto basically a conveyor belt where it's met with the nori. And then the ingredients are hand placed inside, and as it's going down the line, when it gets toward the end of the sushi robot, the conveyor belt actually rolls, if you will, to close the roll. And the roll comes out into about a ten-inch log. And then from there, it's seasoned with the sesame seeds, and after that we have people that actually cut those logs into pieces, and then they're hand placed into the packaging. And then a label is applied, and it goes out to the grocery stores." And convenience stores, gas stations, drug stores, and more.

Schram says Fuji's premade sushi rolls contain no raw fish—only cooked seafood. "It is accepted because a California roll is a California roll," she says. "Whether you buy a prepackaged one or one that's rolled fresh in front of you, it's recognizable. And you know, you can't really screw up a California roll." Schram says Fuji has become the largest supplier of fresh prepackaged sushi in America, selling a dozen different kinds of rolls. They also sell frozen sushi—Walmart has been a customer. And they have another division for fresh-made sushi sold on-site.

But the big dog in the fresh-made sector is another company, Advanced Fresh Concepts, known as AFC, which was recently bought by a Japanese food conglomerate for 257 million dollars. "We've been doing up to a billion in revenue in recent years," says Brian Ishii, whose father started the company in 1986. And he says, "Business has been expanding steadily for thirty-three years." AFC trains new franchisees to make sushi at supermarkets, universities, hospitals, sports stadiums, and other high-traffic locations. The company provides the fish, rice, seaweed, and other ingredients, and splits revenue with both the location and the chef. They recently struck a deal to place sushi bars in some of Amazon's new bricks-and-mortar Amazon Fresh supermarkets. And AFC is now focusing on sustainability of their seafood. "We source it from all over the world," Ishii says. "We're working with a lot of programs and sourcing that's completely sustainable."

In fact, sustainability is becoming a major concern as stocks of fish traditionally used for sushi, like bluefin tuna and freshwater eel, plummet from overfishing and habitat destruction. At Miya's Sushi in New Haven, Connecticut, where everything on the menu is sustainable, from seafood to shore grass, visionary chef Bun Lai has taken his environmental concerns even further. He makes a point of serving invasive species. "Invasive species are species that human beings have brought from one area to another area that they're not indigenous to, and then they wreak havoc on that habitat," he says. "So, by focusing our appetites on these invasive species, then you potentially help restore that habitat that's being hurt by them." Among the invasive species on Lai's menu are varieties of carp, catfish, lionfish, and jellyfish, all of which make terrific sushi. Lai says, "Instead of eating that bluefin tuna, eat that carp instead." Or sushi made with vegetables which, Bai says, actually constitutes the vast majority of what he serves.

Marisa Baggett in Memphis is creating new sushi in the spirit of the old: "To me, traditional sushi isn't about the ingredients so much as it's about the method and using what's fresh and what's seasonal and what's available to you. One of the great things about being in the South is we have this great history of farming, and we have this history of pickling. Pickled vegetables in Japan are huge, especially when it comes to sushi, like the little salads and the pickled vegetables that tend to go in some of the more traditional rolls. I don't know why, but it always just made sense to me from the very beginning, rather than trying to find all these things that may not be available to me, why not use what we have here? Why not use pickled okra? Why not use things that we can get our hands on and pickle them ourselves to use in sushi? It just made sense to me to use what was close and nearby and seasonal. Like pickled green beans and some of the radishes that we can grow. And making a nice little thing with collard greens."

Sasha Issenberg says sushi has never been static. "The fact is, sushi has always changed," he says. "The way it's sold, from outdoor to indoor, the creation of the sushi bar, the types of fish that Japanese people eat, I mean, all of this has changed continuously over hundreds of years, especially over the last two hundred years, and I don't think that Oklahoma's deep-frying sushi is any more dishonest to the history of sushi than Japanese people creating sushi bars because the military government in the 1930s banned street vendors. I think you'll continue seeing people improvise and create in the spirit of deep-fried sushi, addressing to local tastes, local demand, local ingredients, context."

Back at the Ninja Sushi Station in Del City, Oklahoma, where the local favorite is deep-fried, Lucy Guymon and her husband have stopped in to pick up some sushi for her son. She says, "I like how in here it's all cooked up or fried up and not raw. I couldn't eat anything raw like that. But here it's awesome and safe to eat, and even if you don't want the fish you can get a roll with fried chicken." To her, sushi—the way she likes it—is now just another option: "It's not really that much different than buying something like chicken strips or hot dogs from a convenience store, right? That's the way I figure."

Basic Cucumber Roll

Recipe

Equipment

- bamboo sushi rolling mat
- rice paddle, preferably plastic for its nonstick properties
- electric rice cooker
- nonmetallic bowl
- cutting board
- strainer

Ingredients

- 2½ cups short grain rice
- ¾ cup rice vinegar
- cup sugar
- 3 tsp. salt
- 3 tbsp. less than 2½ cups water
- 4 sheets nori (4 x 7 in/10 x 18 cm)
- 1 cucumber, de-seeded and cut into thin strips
- 1 tsp. toasted sesame seeds

Directions

- Place rice in a nonmetallic bowl, cover the rice with water, and swirl carefully by hand. Pour out the water, refill, and repeat three times. Rinse the rice in a fine mesh strainer, then drain it for ten minutes or until the water in the bowl is clear.

- Steam the rice in an electric rice cooker for forty minutes.

- While the rice is cooking, mix together vinegar, sugar, and salt in a nonmetal bowl.

- Place the cooked rice onto a cutting board. Using a rice paddle, fold in the vinegar, sugar, and salt mixture. Cover this with a damp cloth and allow it to cool to room temperature. Do not refrigerate.

- Open a rolling mat with the flat sides of the slats facing up. Place nori on the mat, with the rough side up. Spread a thin layer of rice, leaving a visible border on the long side farthest away. Place one or two cucumber strips atop the rice. Add sesame seeds.

- Pick up the mat and nori from the edge closest to you, roll it over, press down gently to shape it, and repeat this until the roll is closed, seam side down. Cut the roll into six pieces.

The Bagelization of America

It's a chilly Wednesday at Russ & Daughters on the Lower East Side of Manhattan, where they were artisans before artisanal was hip. Each lox and cream cheese on a house-baked bagel is created fresh, the salmon hand-sliced oh-so-slowly, one near-transparent piece at a time. This is the same way things were done after Joel Russ risked everything, traded in his herring pushcart, and opened his store on Orchard Street in 1914, moving it around the corner to the current space on Houston Street nine years later. Three generations later, his great-granddaughter and current co-owner Niki Russ Federman says, "We want our customers who've been coming to Russ & Daughters, eating our food for forty, fifty, sixty years, to feel like, 'Oh, it's the same.' "

And it is. Even behind the counter, where Herman Vargas—who came to New York from the Dominican Republic at the age of fourteen and wields not just a knife, but also an impressive Yiddish vocabulary—has been slicing for nearly forty years. "This is like playing violin," Vargas says as my slicing lesson produces little more than salmon tartare. Still, he keeps trying: "The movement is like symphony, one two, one two," he coaches.

And the concert hall is packed—the coronavirus crisis of 2020 is still a year away—and today's lunch hour is a constant stream of twenty or twenty-five customers at a time, no tables, just takeout. Waiting impatiently, but resignedly, Al Bornstein says he's been coming here for more than twenty-five years "because there is absolutely no place better than this with smoked fish in the world." Russ & Daughters is what is called an appetizing store, providing generations of Jewish New Yorkers (and many non-Jews once the secret got out) with pickled, salted, or smoked fish—herring, lox, whitefish, sturgeon, and more—alongside pickles, sour tomatoes, dried fruits, halvah (a sweet dessert made from sesame paste), and tins of caviar. Of course, the assortment was neither so wide nor anywhere so luxurious at first.

The original customers, desperately poor Jewish immigrants, were after the only thing they could afford, herring. At five cents apiece or three for a dime, two herring and a loaf of bread could be stretched to feed a family twice. First, the herring would be rubbed on the bread, leaving behind enough fat for that to become dinner number one. The fish itself would be dinner number two. Lox, which was salt-preserved salmon, was much more expensive—seven to nine cents a quarter pound—and on the rare occasion a customer bought some, it was almost always a tiny piece called a halbe fierte, Yiddish for half of a quarter. That meant two one-ounce strips divided among everyone in the family and eaten on dark bread with butter or the rendered chicken fat called schmaltz. It was only as the next generation reached adulthood and inched into at least the lower middle class that the full splendors of appetizing became affordable, at least for special occasions.

Early on, Russ & Daughters (Joel Russ had no sons) was just one among dozens of appetizing stores and other Jewish food stores on the Lower East Side, which in the early twentieth century was the most densely populated neighborhood on earth, the first place many immigrants of all nationalities landed after passing through Ellis Island. It was a claustrophobic, choking environment—tenements overstuffed with humanity, laundry hanging over every alley, streets filled with vendors, horse-carts, kids playing a combination of tag and hide-and-seek called ringolevio, people shouting from window to window and down to the street in German, Italian, Yiddish, Russian, and more. Between 1900 and 1924 alone, more than a million Jews fleeing Europe ended up here.

But as second and third-generation Jews moved up and out—to Brooklyn, Queens, the Bronx, or the Upper West Side—and over succeeding decades, as the neighborhood descended into a cesspool of drugs, crime, and violence, almost all of the Jewish food stores, not just appetizing but also delis, knish stores, and dairy restaurants, shut down. Russ & Daughters stubbornly fought for their livelihood. "My parents, to their credit, kept the door open when everyone was like, 'Close the door!' " Federman says. By the seventies, customers felt like they were shopping at their own risk. "Someone would stay in the car, leave the car running," Federman says, "the other person would run in, get their appetizing, run out, and leave. And my father, he worked so hard for every single customer because he was so afraid that people would not keep coming." But enough did. And eventually, developers started remaking the area. These days, it's reenergized, with high-rises, galleries, coffee shops, and homes for young singles and families, full of tourists and customers.

On this day, the crowd includes Asian tourists and Parisian expat Barbara Capellie, who sounds like a real New Yorker when she says simply, "It's the best place to buy some salmon. It's the best." There's a hipster with an abnormally wide soul patch and a woman with an Eastern European accent and shocking copper-red hair. Near the end of the counter, retired stockbroker Marc Vosen tells me that he stops in whenever he visits the city from Cleveland, even on the way to lunch. "I love sable," he says. "Sometimes I'm going next door to Katz's [famed delicatessen] to meet my buddies. I'll just pop in here real quick, get me four little slices of sable, and have it for an appetizer."

And there's longtime customer Bob Bozic, an imposing former heavyweight boxer, eager to open his wallet to show me a picture of him with heavyweight champion Larry Holmes, who broke Bozic's nose and punched out three of his teeth, but couldn't knock him out when they fought at Madison Square Garden in 1973. Bozic's good with a story. Waiting in line, he paints a picture of the old days, when he felt lucky to share Sunday brunches with Jewish mobster and boxing bigwig Champ Segal. "He'd sit in bed," Bozic reminisces. "Him and his friends would put chairs, we put plates on the bed. They were ordering from Russ & Daughters and they'd have the smoked fish and everything like that. And they'd sit around and tell stories."

Today, Bozic's waiting for an order of smoked whitefish, a surprise gift for some friends upstate. It's a big seller here, but the signature order is the classic lox or smoked salmon and cream cheese on a bagel. Not just any bagel. Russ & Daughters makes their own, two-hundred-dozen a day, triple that on holidays, each bagel hand-rolled, boiled, and baked in the traditional way, on burlap-covered wooden planks in a rotating deck oven with six deep shelves. Some first-time customers order those bagels with cream cheese alone, no fish, a kind of gateway shmear. After ten years behind the counter, Johanna Shipman says, "At first our food is strange and foreign and then, eventually, you've heard about it enough times that you're like, 'Oh, I'll give it a shot.' "

And so many have, not just at Russ & Daughters of course, that lox and bagels—especially bagels—have become more than a Jewish or even a New York food. They are now American. They're sold at McDonald's, Starbucks, Panera Bread, and Dunkin' Donuts, which claims to sell the most. There are bagel chains such as Einstein Brothers and Bruegger's, owned, along with several others, by the same company headquartered in Luxembourg. There are mom-and-pop bagel shops in all fifty states. Murray Lender, whose Lenders frozen bagels would revolutionize the industry, called it the "bagelization of America." Here's how it happened.

In the nineteenth century, when Jews from all over Eastern Europe began streaming into America to escape poverty and anti-Semitism, the bagel came with them, a culinary stowaway that historians trace back as far as the early seventeenth century in Poland. Maria Balinska, who wrote *The Bagel: The Surprising History of a Modest Bread*, says it was a little piece of home in a terrifying new world. "They're having their bagel with their butter, or their bagel with their cup of tea" she says. "That was just part of the culture."

By 1900, there were seventy bakeries on the Lower East Side of New York, now making their bagels bigger, with smaller holes, suitable for slicing and shmearing with butter, schmaltz, or that newly marketed wonder-food, cream cheese, and topped with lox, salmon preserved in salt, for those who could afford it.

Hollywood legend Mel Brooks remembers growing up poor in Brooklyn, as Melvin Kaminsky, when a bagel with cream cheese and lox was something very special: "It was a treat," he recalled over the phone from his office in Los Angeles. "It could only be once a week, usually on a Sunday. I was just, I think, five years old and I remember loving it. But by the forties, things were a little better after the war and people had a little more money and you could have bagels and lox on a Tuesday." While non-Jews in New York discovered the bagel by the fifties, most of the rest of America—with the exception of a few big cities with significant Jewish populations—didn't know they existed. Until the word began trickling out.

Maria Balinska says that as the sixties approached, "You begin to get accounts of bagels, and what they are, talked about in media." A *Saturday Evening Post* article in February of 1958 defined bagels as "doughnut shaped rolls boiled, then baked, to munchy firmness" and suggested giving bagels, lox, and cream cheese a try. A September 1961 issue of *Look Magazine*, with three-year-old Caroline Kennedy on the cover, included lox and bagel meal suggestions and a recipe for making bagels at home. In May of 1963, *McCall's* ran a feature explaining bagels and lox and listing celebrities said to love them, including Jackie Gleason, Sophie Tucker, Mike Wallace, Alan King, and Mitch Miller. And Balinska says, "That goes hand in hand with Jewish comedians being on television, using bagels as props, using bagels as jokes, and so it's like a perfect storm." She cites Milton Berle joking that his family bought day-old bagels and had to hammer the butter on. And Woody Allen did a bit about a distant island where sex was casual, but food was naughty, and a girl, offered cream cheese with her bagels, snaps, "I don't do that kind of thing." But if a comedian joking about bagels made people want to try one, most Americans were out of luck. With bagel bakeries in only a handful of cities, there was no national supply and nowhere near enough skilled bakers to step up and create one. That would require a technological breakthrough, which arrived in 1962.

That is when former junior high school shop teacher Daniel Thompson patented an automatic bagel making machine, which vastly increased production and speed, turning out as many as 4,800 bagels an hour. He leased the first one to the Lender brothers, Murray, Marvin, and Sam, who ran one of the first bagel bakeries outside New York City, in New Haven, Connecticut. And they began doing something else no one had done before, freezing their bagels and shipping them to places where people had never seen one.

"To take a Jewish product and introduce it to the non-Jewish world takes a lot of creativity, a lot of money," says Marvin Lender, at seventy-eight, the last surviving brother. "We were advertising when we didn't have a penny. We borrowed money to do it, but it was the only way we could introduce the product to a segment of the population that didn't even know what a bagel was." They added bagel flavors never seen on the Lower East Side of New York, such as raisin and honey. And, Lender says, "We got very lucky. We became an alternative to white bread; people were beginning to appreciate ethnic products, i.e. French bread, Italian bread, pizza. And probably the most important is that the frozen aspect gave us two things, unlimited distribution and we caught the wave of frozen foods, which in the sixties was just getting off the ground." But even as America embraced Lender's bagels, buying sixty-five-million-dollars-worth in 1984, traditional bagel lovers demonized them. The bagels weren't chewy enough, they complained, or crunchy enough.

Marvin Lender says, of course they weren't: "I agree with them. The bagels that we were making were quite different than what my father made. It's hard to replicate the same quality of anything when you're mass producing something [and] the bagel that my father made was not a bagel that you could market outside of the

Jewish community." Simply too crunchy, he says, and too chewy. Too big a leap from Wonder Bread and dinner rolls.

Purists blame the automatic bagel maker for the softening of the bagel, saying it only worked with a watered-down dough. Thompson's sons, who now run the company, say their father's machine could handle any dough, but other companies' equipment that mixed and cut the dough to feed into the machine could not. Still, automation, quickly adopted not just by Lender's but also by a raft of new competitors, unquestionably produced a softer bagel. And that is now the standard almost everywhere, as is a sweeter taste and a raft of stabilizers and preservatives.

The bagel revolution the Lenders created is all around us today, from individual bagel joints to bagel chains like Einstein Bros. and Bruegger's. From fast-food joints like McDonald's and Dunkin' Donuts to massive grocery store suppliers like Thomas's English Muffins, Sarah Lee, and a huge multinational food company, Bimbo Bakeries, which now owns Lender's. These days, the bagel's meteoric rise has hit a plateau—growing, but not astronomically— yet at such a high level that it is firmly established as one of America's favorite breakfasts, especially with millions of people eating in their cars. Maria Balinksa says, "It's very convenient. It lends itself to grab and go, and it doesn't crumble. I'd also think it's just a product that you have an affection for." Along with the ascension of the bagel, came the shocking rise of its sidekick, lox, or more specifically smoked salmon, also known as Nova. For many would-be bagel-eaters, lox had long been a bridge too far. But slowly, millions of Americans crossed it, now eating more than one-billion-dollars-worth of smoked salmon annually, and consumption keeps growing.

Much of it comes from one fourth-generation family business in Brooklyn, Acme Smoked Fish Corporation, founded by Harry Brownstein, who emigrated from Russia in the early twentieth century. He started small, as a "wagon jobber," buying fish wholesale from some of the dozens of smokehouses operating in Brooklyn and Queens and selling them to appetizing stores from a horse drawn wagon. His great-grandson, Adam Caslow, one of Acme's current owners, says, "He was just struggling to get by in his little sales route and his dream was to open up his own smokehouse. He actually wasn't able to start Acme until the very end of his career in 1954." The next generations fought hard to make and keep Acme a major player. Caslow says his father and uncle, running the company in the eighties, came up with an aggressive strategy: "Back in the day when all the fish was wild, they would front some of these fisherman money for nets and equipment, so that they would be the first ones to get access to the fish. There was only so much fish that was allocated from Seattle to the northeast. That was a pivotal competitive advantage of getting access; there wasn't enough fish for everyone."

But the future was not in being a banker for a boat captain. It was in creating a reliable supply of fish. As salmon farming proved practical in the eighties, Acme embraced it in a big way. Almost all of the salmon they now buy is sustainably farmed in Norway and Chile. And advances in vacuum packaging and automated production opened up an entirely new market, the grocery store. Much as Lender's gave America the bagel, Acme gave America smoked salmon. And Caslow says the market just keeps growing everywhere, including places not traditionally thought of as Jewish. "It's becoming a staple of the aisle," he says. "For example, you may go to Wal-Mart in Alabama and they're going to have smoked salmon on their shelf there." His sister and Acme co-owner, Emily

Gindi, still isn't sure why. "Which came first?" she wonders. "Did it become available in other markets through stores like Costco and therefore people who didn't have access to it before tried it, or did those stores bring it in because people wanted it?"

Patrick Wemberly, standing in a long line at Acme's Brooklyn headquarters, says, "I didn't know that I liked lox until I found this place." Wemberly, who is not Jewish, and his ten-month-old daughter, Issa, in her stroller, are nearing the front of the line, which now stretches out the door and down Gem Street on this "Fish Friday," the one day a week Acme is open to retail customers (though the format would later be modified to curbside pickup during the COVID pandemic). Just a bit behind them, Judi Weinstock, who clearly knows her appetizing, says she's here for, "the best, freshest smoked fish in New York for the best price. It's delicious, connects you with the tribe, harks back to childhood experiences with your family." And, she points out, this is a very diverse crowd. "You come here, you can hear Japanese, Polish, anything and it's great." Just a few feet away, Mie Roppondi, who is from Japan but lives in Manhattan, says she comes here for smoked salmon about once a month "because it's very tasty, very good," and reminds her of fish back home.

While customers do their shopping in one room at the front, work goes on throughout the rest of the building on a host of products— whitefish, sable, sturgeon, herring and, of course, many varieties of salmon, from lox simply brined in salt to smoked salmon from varying locales, brined and then smoked in different ways. Workers shuttle racks loaded with five or six hundred pounds of fish, tend to bins and barrels of fish being cured, run whitefish through de-scaling machines and salmon through slicers, and stuff plastic pouches with Nova and lox headed for the supermarket. One crew is unloading forty-thousand pounds of frozen whole salmon from Chile. Four men at a stainless-steel table are slicing their way through a pile of wild Alaskan Red King Salmon. With a single stroke, they cut each fish right down the middle, then debone and trim it, and send it on for brining or smoking in room-sized smokers fueled, surprisingly, by the same small wood chips used in a backyard grill. The floors are wet, the air is humid, but the slog is worth it. At the end of my tour, I'm handed a piece of fresh lox, the original salty kind, right off the line.

This is no longer Acme's main plant. They have more heavily automated facilities in North Carolina, Florida, and Chile. But this is where they prepare specific products for their pickiest customers, including Russ & Daughters on the Lower East Side, their traditional uptown Manhattan competitors, Zabar's and Barney Greengrass, and an out-of-towner, Kenny & Ziggy's, a legendary delicatessen run by a transplanted New Yorker in Houston, Texas. And while these and other icons, like Langer's and Canter's in Los Angeles and Zingerman's in Ann Arbor, are keeping tradition alive, a new generation of restaurateurs is joining them. Says Caslow, "What's interesting in recent years has been this renaissance of bagels and smoked salmon that has spawned these great innovative restaurant concepts in smaller cities." In places like Austin, Denver, and Portland (both Maine and Oregon), as well as in traditional deli cities like New York and Los Angeles, a growing number of chefs and bakers are getting passionate about bagels and lox (and other traditionally Jewish food). New twists on one hand and a return to tradition on the other.

In Denver, Rosenberg's Bagels & Delicatessen smokes their own salmon and hard-to-find New York appetizing specialties sturgeon and sable, and makes their own bagels, treating the water they're made with to mimic the mineral content of water from New York City (even though debate over the contribution of local water to the quality of New York bagels remains unresolved). In Seattle, Westman's Bagel and Coffee dusts some of its fresh-baked bagels with English Maldon sea salt, makes its own vegan cream cheese, and offers salmon caviar shmears. In Washington, DC, Call Your Mother deli tops bagels with za'atar, the Middle Eastern spice mix, and offers a candied salmon cream cheese.

"The way I look at it [is] more akin to the craft beer movement and artisanal chocolate and artisanal cheese," says Maria Balinksa. "There's a real interest in products that are made by hand, that are not as standardized. And you can see that with bread generally, of course, but I think there's a particular interest in bagels."

Pete Linde and his wife, Janna, got into the artisanal bagel business five years ago. Pete, an automotive engineer had been transferred to Kansas City by the Ford Motor Company twenty-three years earlier. The good news? He met and married Janna there. The bad news? They were living in a bagel desert. "There was literally not a legitimate bagel to be found in this town," he says. "Just chains and fast-food bagels. Here I'm a transplanted New York Jew craving a bagel, thinking, God, somebody's got to do this because I want one. But, I mean, you've spent enough time in Kansas City to know it's not the most Jewish place in the world, right?"

At first Janna, a non-Jewish Kansas City native, did not understand the depths of his pain. But then, they visited New York together. "It was romantic, it really was," she says, laughing. "We got our bagels and our shmear and our whitefish and our Nova and we sat on the blanket in Central Park and I took a bite into it and I couldn't believe it. I was like, 'What the hell? This is crazy good.' " They began to nurture a fantasy of one day opening a bagel bakery of their own.

Pete says six years later Janna convinced him to make it real. "She said, 'You know what? There's no time like the present. Let's just get on it and do it.' "

Not that either of them had any idea how. "We knew you had to boil them," Pete says. "We knew you had to bake them. And that was about as far as our knowledge went." Janna went searching for equipment while Pete scoured the internet for recipes and guidance and, on his seventy-third attempt, he says he finally got it right. "I did my one-dozen batch at eleven o'clock at night when our son was asleep and they came out of the oven, they looked good, they tore the right way, and we bit into them and we were just like, 'Wow, we have a recipe.' By that point, the bakery space had already been leased and we had equipment coming in. So, we effectively were building a bakery before we had a bagel recipe."

If that sounds like a crazy way to get into business, they named the company appropriately. The Yiddish word for crazy is meshuggah and their company is Meshuggah Bagels. Janna says the day they opened was chaos: "We were literally like the Soup Nazi off of *Seinfeld*. People were lined up two blocks down the street the entire day. It never let up." Still, Pete says, there was a learning curve: "It took quite a bit of education. First time in, it's just bagel and plain cream cheese and they didn't want to go anywhere near a piece of smoked salmon or a whitefish salad or anything like that. But, little by little by little, they saw the transplanted East Coasters buying them or we would just give samples, and after the first six months people that had previously been plain bagel, plain cream cheese [were ordering] everything bagel, Nova, onions, tomatoes, capers like they'd been living in New York their whole life."

As for that Nova, Pete and Janna won't name their supplier, but say they get all of their fish from New York. And they are pragmatic enough about local tastes to offer a variety of bagel flavors not originally found on the Lower East Side, from chocolate chip to lemon poppy seed. From one location, they've grown to four, Pete says, selling 7,800 bagels a week. "The fact that this town supports four stores for bagels and cream cheese and smoked fish just was an incredible surprise to us," he says. "Something we never could've done a business study on and predicted."

As for the future? Pete and Janna have done extremely well, as have many of their counterparts in other cities. Though not as explosively as in the eighties and nineties, bagel sales continue to grow. More than two hundred million Americans are now eating more than a billion dollars' worth of bagels annually. Everything Bagels in Soldotna, Alaska, offers reindeer sausage in a cheddar bacon bagel. Atlanta's General Muir Appetizing and Delicatessen, a two-time James Beard Award semi-finalist, tops one of their nova and cream cheese bagels with avocado, grapefruit, cucumber, onion, and dill. Forage Market in Lewiston, Maine, makes what *Saveur* says may be the best bagels in the country. Original Bagel, one of several companies selling par-baked frozen bagels for local bagel shops to warm up and serve as if fresh, is producing two million bagels a week. Russ & Daughters now has four locations, including two eat-in restaurants and a major production facility and takeout counter anchoring a major new commercial development in the Brooklyn Navy Yard. And the restaurant selling the most bagels to consumers all over America remains Dunkin' Donuts.

Lox, Eggs, and Onions

Another way to enjoy smoked salmon with a bagel, a classic New York brunch favorite. The name is traditional, but these days, it is almost always made with smoked salmon, not the much-saltier lox.

Ingredients

- 1–2 tbsp. unsalted butter
- 1 large onion, finely chopped
- 3–4 oz. smoked salmon, cut into bite sized pieces
- 8 eggs, well beaten
- salt and pepper to taste
- bagels
- butter or cream cheese for bagels as desired

Directions

- In a medium nonstick pan, melt butter over medium heat. Add onions, stirring frequently, until soft and translucent. Add salt and pepper to taste. Reduce the heat to low, add smoked salmon and stir for about three minutes. Add beaten eggs, stirring continuously for two-and-a-half to three minutes until desired consistency is reached. Pair with lightly toasted bagels with a shmear of cream cheese or a pat of butter.

Wings-N-Things

Sahlen Field, home of the minor league Buffalo Bisons, holds a groundbreaking place in baseball history. It is the first of what are called "retro parks," incorporating design elements reminiscent of stadiums built as far back as the twenties. Columns. Balustrades. It's a style that was later used in a succession of major league parks, most notably, Camden Yards in Baltimore. Sahlen Field is also one of the largest ballparks in the minors. And today, it is packed, but on the field, no one is chasing fly balls. No, on this cloudless end-of-summer day, they're chasing chicken wings. Thousands of people—more than fifty thousand over this Labor Day weekend—hustling, or ambling, from booth to booth to sample more than a hundred varieties of wings, here at the 2019 Buffalo Chicken Wing Festival. Everything from peanut butter and jelly wings, to maple syrup and habanero, to something called chicken wing soup. Everywhere, cheeks, chins, fingers, and shirts are covered with a slick layer of sauce in some shade of orange or brown—there's only so much a wet towelette can do. People are juggling plates filled with wings, bones, or both, many tearing up and sniffling when wings touted as "hot" exceed their billing. With the booths arranged around the perimeter of the field, long lines stretch from each like spokes from a wheel and converge in the center. The smell in the air is a mixture of tangy and sweet. The underlying soundtrack is the sizzle of dozens of deep fryers. Trash cans overflow with napkins that didn't quite do their job.

Surveying everything is a tall, fiftyish man in khaki shorts, a black baseball hat, and a black T-shirt emblazoned with "Wing King."

That's Drew Cerza, who started this event eighteen years ago. And as would be expected of someone who calls himself the Wing King and has been known to dress up in a red cape and a chicken-wing-shaped crown, Cerza's enthusiasm for chicken wings is boundless. "They're fun, they're exciting, they're passionate," he says. "They're an entertaining food to eat. They're not boring. There are so many different varieties of them. You've got an option. You can do a flat. You can do a drumstick. You can dip in blue cheese. You can do whatever you want, so it's almost like a workout."

And as athletic trainers like to say about workouts, "No pain, no gain." Some of the wings offered here are spicy beyond belief. "Hot's better, hot's the best," says owner Mark Ebeling of Danny's South restaurant, answering questions as he tries to solve an electrical problem at his booth. "Our most popular sauce that we do in the restaurant, it's called Tailgater," he says. "It's a hot sauce with Cajun spices, and then we're just doing one we're starting, we call it maple fire. It's got maple syrup and hot sauce. It's very good."

Wing King Cerza says, "Everybody's got different tastes. So, whether you like a sweet wing, a spicy wing, a sweet and spicy, a hot wing, there's everything. I mean, I wouldn't even know where to start. But there's, it's surprising. The wing that you wouldn't think you'd like, a lot of times is the wing you really like. So, you gotta step out of the box and just explore."

As James Pullano did. A young guy with a beard and a broad smile, holding a beer, wearing a backward baseball cap and a shark tooth necklace, he describes the blueberry balsamic wing he tried as "a little bit different than your traditional wing sauce, which is a bit tangy, spicy. It was more sweet and savory, but that's part of the beauty of this is that you have all kinds of varieties." And best of show? For him, it's a wing from a restaurant in Great Britain. "I've got to say my favorite that I've had today is the Woof Woof, the wing over from the UK place," he says. "It's all made from chili peppers and stuff. It's definitely a little bit different style, almost tastes like it had a curry flavor to it, really good."

Lisa Gentile's inspiration was Mexican. She won first place in the festival's Amateur Wing Creative Sauce-Off with al pastor wings. "I got the idea because we eat al pastor tacos," she says. "And so, I tried to make that sauce into a wing sauce, and it's just different types of chiles, and anchovy paste, and pineapple, and stuff." All in all, there are more than a hundred different kinds of wings available at the various booths here today, a far cry from the single recipe that started it all.

The story goes that Buffalo wings were invented at that city's Anchor Bar back in 1964. At his booth at the festival, Anchor CEO Mark Dempsey repeats that claim. "They're the original. We invented the wing. So we know what they're supposed to be," he says. "Always fresh, never frozen, never breaded. That's a true Buffalo chicken wing. And the secret's in the sauce, the flavoring in the sauce, just the right measure of cayenne, vinegar, garlic, salt." But the story of their origin is muddled. Frank Bellissimo, original owner of the Anchor Bar, told people the bar received a delivery of chicken wings by mistake, so his wife Teressa Bellissimo found a creative use for them—cutting off and discarding the tips, then cutting the wings in half, deep-frying them, tossing them in Frank's brand hot sauce and butter (and perhaps a few seasonings), and serving them with celery sticks and the blue cheese dressing the Anchor served on salads. But Frank and Teressa's son Dom told a different story. He said he and some friends were hanging out at the bar late on a Friday night, at a time when most Catholics in Buffalo would not eat meat on a Friday. Dom said he asked his mother to whip something up for his group to snack on after midnight, when meat would again be legal. As he told it, that's when she invented the now-legendary creation. All three have passed away and the question remains unresolved. Either way, Teressa Bellissimo gets the credit.

Yet, another restaurateur, also deceased, claimed he was the first to fry chicken wings in Buffalo, also in the sixties. John Young ran a restaurant called Wings and Things (no relation to any later chain). Born and raised in Stockton, Alabama, Young pointed out that there was a long tradition of eating chicken wings in the African American community, and his daughter Lina says that clearly included her father's family. "His mother and father raised them on chicken wings," she says. "I would imagine probably like most Black people from the South, they were eating all parts of the chicken. Gizzards, liver. The wing. I don't think they threw away too much of the chicken pieces." Unlike those served at the Anchor Bar, Young's wings were breaded, served whole, and coated with what he called Mumbo sauce, a tomato-based mixture that was at least somewhat sweet. His daughter Lina knows the recipe well. She happened to be frying up a batch for relatives when we talked by phone. "The original wing was a whole wing dipped in red Mumbo sauce," she says. "And many Buffalonians, probably including the Anchor Bar, knew about [it]. Now, it could be that they were the first to cut the wing and serve it with blue cheese. That could be. And that is what most people know as the Buffalo chicken wing. But the original way Buffalo chicken wings were sold in Buffalo was whole wings with Mumbo sauce."

Not everyone accepts that timeline, but *Buffalo News* food editor Andrew Z. Galarneau, who's likely written more about chicken wings than anyone else on earth, is convinced. "It's backed up by looking at the city directories, and seeing that this restaurant existed before the 'blessed event' at the Anchor Bar," he says. "So, it's pretty conclusive, to me at least." Yet it was the wings as served at the Anchor Bar—cut in pieces, tossed in hot sauce and butter, no breading, served with celery and blue cheese—that would become a national phenomenon. The Anchor's Mark Dempsey says, "It's not that Teressa invented the actual chicken wing. She just invented the chicken wing that has the Buffalo sauce on it, right. The Buffalo version." Now, he says, "You can't go too many places without finding some type of chicken wing on the menu."

They have become a staple. At more than 40 percent of the top five hundred restaurant chains. At so-called fast-casual restaurants such as Applebee's, Chili's, The Cheesecake Factory, TGI Fridays, Ruby Tuesday, and more. At virtually every pizza chain, including the market leaders, Domino's and Pizza Hut. At local family-owned restaurants of all kinds. At bars, especially sports bars such as Dave & Busters and Duffy's Sports Grill. At strip clubs. Even at high-end restaurants.

And, of course, at a variety of chains specializing in wings, including Buffalo Wild Wings, the leader in that category, their biggest competitor, Wingstop, and many others. And while they don't have wings in their name, Hooters calls itself "The Original American Wing Joint." One of the founding partners, Gil DiGiannantonio, says it all began with a fateful road trip from the Tampa Bay area, where he lived, to a tiny restaurant serving wings in Fort Lauderdale: "We bought a bottle of Smirnoff vodka and a case of Stroh's beer. And the four or five of us jumped in the van and we drove all the way down, had lunch, turned around and drove all the way back. And we said, 'Hell, we can do this.' " So, they did. "The wings took off," he says. "It just exploded."

One of the other original partners, L.D. Stewart says, "Nobody ate chicken wings. Hell. You eat the chicken breasts, the legs, the thighs. But nobody ate the chicken wings and as a result I could get them real cheap. Nowadays you can hardly buy the damn things."

In fact, demand is so high that wings today are actually more expensive than chicken breasts. Still, customers expect them to be inexpensive, often less than a dollar apiece. In late 2020, Wingstop began testing bone-in thighs as a possible menu option to ease the price pressure. Noted food industry analyst David Portalatin says, "They are so popular, in fact, that there are some supply chain issues. Because the good Lord only produces a bird that has two wings. So now you'll see the onset of something like boneless wings, which really means it's not a wing at all. It's formed together from some other chicken parts, but we're going to call it wings anyway."

Bone-in or boneless, breaded or bare, wings are packed away by Americans at an astonishing rate, especially on Super Bowl Sunday, when the total number of wings sold in America—technically wing segments, either the drumette, the part that looks like a miniature leg, also known as a drummie or the flat—approaches one-point-four billion.

And the folks at the Wings Cafe in the gentrifying Kansas City, Missouri, neighborhood of Westport are doing their part. Hours before the Kansas City Chiefs come from behind to defeat the San Francisco Forty-Niners in Super Bowl LIV, the crew is frying and saucing nonstop. "We have been slammed since this morning," says Charito Redwood, whose husband, Lee, is co-owner of the restaurant. "Bone-in and bone out. Chicken strips. They want it all." As she talks, she keeps an eye on the swinging kitchen doors, which barely stop moving as the staff rushes orders out. One customer, anxious to get home to a houseful of guests, is picking up an order of 150.

Back in the kitchen, it's a well-choreographed assembly line—flour, fry, then toss in sauce. No chaos. Everyone knows what to do. Recently hired Derion Drew, young, gangly, wearing black rubber gloves and a black apron covered with white smudges, is working the flouring station. Over and over, he grabs wings from a white plastic bucket to his right, dredges them, one in each hand in a bowl full of flour, shakes off the excess, puts them in a wire basket to his left, and drops the basket into boiling oil. It's repetitive work, he's on his feet for hours—shifts have been extended to keep up with the rush—but this is a special day. "This is my first Super Bowl." He says. "It's exciting."

Out front at a table with friends, Jordan Delacruz explains, "Wings and football and beer is just a thing." And Delacruz is pragmatic. "It's finger food," he says, "And they have plenty of paper towels here." The glazed and gooey selection on the table—and in their mouths and on their faces—includes hot Buffalo wings, sweet Thai, Texas cowboy, and garlic parmesan, just a handful of the twenty-two flavors offered here, done breaded or bare, and bone-in or boneless, a far cry from the single Anchor Bar original.

But even the Anchor has accepted that wing-lovers these days demand variety. "Nowadays, it's more than throwing raw wings in a fryer and cooking them for a few minutes and putting some sauce on it," says CEO Mark Dempsey. "People are ordering wings like they order steak. 'I'll have a steak medium rare. I'll have a steak well done.' We've got levels of crispiness. We've got levels of heat. We've got dry rubs now. The Anchor Bar serves about twenty different flavors of wings, of sauces or rubs."

Portalatin says, "We have this trend in cuisine for several years now around both heat, as well as global flavors, and there's a lot of intersection there. So, wings, in a sense, is the template for a lot of experimentation, and exploration around both heat and different cuisines and flavors." Wing menus are full of international flavors such as teriyaki, Thai, curry, adobo, Caribbean jerk, Korean, and more. And in fact, wings have long been a part of many other cuisines, especially in Asia. Thailand for example. Vietnam, China, and Korea. The Bonchon chain, which sells Korean-style wings—and the rest of the chicken too—is up to three hundred locations and growing.

James Beard award winning chef Andy Ricker began selling Vietnamese style wings at his Pok Pok restaurant in Portland in 2005. "I became aware of them during a trip to Vietnam," he says. "I stopped at a Bia Hoi stand, which is a little fresh beer spot on the street in Saigon. And that was one of the things on the menu and I thought, wow, that was fucking amazing." He says there's a similar dish in Thailand. "You just take some fish sauce, some chicken wings, and you kind of rub them with fish sauce and then you throw them into the deep fryer without any breading or flour or batter or anything. You just deep fry them until they're crispy as hell. So that's the real thing, you find that often at drinking establishments as a snack."

In America, the wings are often on the menu right next to a selection of other deep-fried finger food favorites, like the onion rings, poppers, or mozzarella sticks that Americans scarf up by the ton. At bars, restaurants, at home watching the big game, even as the country seemingly grows more and more aware of diet and health. "People talk quite the game," says Pete Kerr, Vice President of Sales at Fry Foods, one of the country's largest producers of frozen appetizers and bar food. "They go to the gym instead of going to lunch, and then they go to happy hour and enjoy some of my mozzarella sticks. I love them for that."

For restaurants, this food category is a delight. Almost everything goes straight from freezer to deep fryer. "It's just cheaper to do it that way," says the General Manager of a large chain restaurant in a major city. "You're not paying somebody a bunch of money to have to make it. They don't have to be particularly skilled." He says the process requires as little thinking as possible: "We even have timers on the fryers. It's got automatic arms that raise and lower to allow you just to throw whatever it is in a basket, hit a button, three-and-a-half minutes, four minutes later, it pops up, put it on a plate, send it out."

The combination of deep-frying and salt can be irresistible. And so can the feel of simply biting in. Pioneering food preference researcher Dr. Paul Rozin says, "We almost certainly have an innate desire for fatty textures," and for contrast. "One of the things about mozzarella sticks, for Americans at least, is that they have texture contrast, a soft center, so does pizza by the way, and a crispy outside. That seems to be very appealing to many people."

The mozzarella stick first became popular in the seventies and eighties. It was one of the first finger food items on the menu at Applebee's. Now, it is everywhere. Some trace its history all the way back to a recipe in a fifteenth century French guidebook for housewives, but unlike wings, they have no specific origin story here, no tale of a specific chef creating them in a "eureka" moment.

There's just something about molten cheese inside a crispy crust. Another of America's deep-fried favorites is the jalapeño popper, likely descended from a Mexican dish, stuffed peppers called chile rellenos. The poppers served at Ruby Tuesday restaurants made it into Mick Jagger's monologue when he hosted Saturday Night Live in 2012. "They asked me if I would come along to their grand openings and sing the theme song *Ruby Tuesday* for a thousand dollars and a lifetime supply of jalapeño poppers," he told the audience. "I passed up on that offer, and not a day goes by that I don't regret that."

Cheeseless but immensely popular is the onion ring. Pete Kerr of Fry Foods says it's their bestseller: "We do well over a hundred million pounds of onions a year." Most accounts credit the introduction of onion rings to the Pig Stand drive in chain in Texas in the 1920s, though a recipe for onions fried in lard was published in a popular English cookbook in 1802. A close cousin of the ring, the "bloomin' onion," was introduced by Outback Steakhouse in the late eighties.

Potato skins became an unlikely hit when TGI Fridays added them to their menu in 1974. Founding CEO Dan Scoggin says, "We had a thing in our test kitchen that if you deep fry it, put cheese on it, you can sell anything." Even leftovers. "When we were developing them, we had a lot of our management saying, 'That's ridiculous. That's the part of the potato that you're supposed to throw away, who would eat a potato skin?' " Millions of people, it turned out.

And not just the skins. Tater Tots were invented by the Ore-Ida company in the fifties to use the bits of potato left over when they made their main product, French fries. These days, tots are served in countless ways—on top of pizza; on nachos; and topped with lobster, smoked pork, fried chicken, chili, and more. Americans eat nearly two hundred thousand pounds of tots every day, seventy million pounds a year. And no, they aren't all "Tater Tots," since Ore-Ida owns the name.

And there are taquitos, battered mushrooms, fried pickles, nachos—okay, the whole sloppy platter isn't fried, but the chips are—almost anything that can be fried and grabbed has made it onto someone's menu, including one item that became so trendy the *New York Times* used its rapid rise as the yardstick for measuring the impact of other food trends. Calamari in Italian, calamar in French and Spanish, kalamaraki in Greek, squid has long been a popular food in the Mediterranean. It is prepared many ways there, including grilled, charred, roasted, sautéed, and of course, fried. But for decades it did not enter the mainstream American diet, served at only a handful of places, such as Randazzo's Clam Bar by the water in the Sheepshead Bay section of Brooklyn, a brick-fronted restaurant with a massive red neon sign in the shape of a lobster hanging from the roof. They've been serving calamari—galamah in the local Italian American dialect—since 1959, long before other restaurateurs were convinced to try it. It was Helen Randazzo's family recipe. Her grandson Michael Geraci says, "The fishermen would come in off the boats after going out and before they headed back out. They would come for a snack or something to eat before they would go back out on their next run. So, she called it a fishermen snack. It was galamah cut up, floured and fried, and then a little bit of her tomato sauce on top." Though the fishermen back then did more than just eat it. "It was bait," Geraci says. "It was never really considered something for food until it became popularized with the sauce." Actually, for most of America, squid would remain nothing more than fish bait for at least another twenty years.

But when the fishing industry faced a serious and growing problem, calamari became their "Hail Mary" pass. In the seventies and eighties, limits imposed on the overfishing of flounder and cod threatened the livelihoods of fishermen who worked the waters off Long Island. So, a food and agriculture research and support program from Cornell University, soon joined by state and federal agencies, began promoting squid as a replacement catch. Assistance funds were provided. The effort went nationwide. Restaurateurs were advised to market this potentially off-putting dish as the international-sounding calamari, not the stomach-turning squid. Afraid no one would try a full plate of rings and tentacles, they began serving it as an appetizer and stumbled onto an incredible success. Suddenly, nothing was trendier than an order of calamari. From singles bars to chain restaurants, family places to fine dining. And what could have been a fad became an unlikely menu staple, another freezer-to-fryer stalwart. The *New York Times* created the Fried Calamari Index to measure the lifespan of any new food trend. Of course, calamari itself never went away. Says Geraci, "It's come a long way from something that people didn't consider food."

It's an essential part of a favorite American food group that never made it into the nutrition pyramid, deep-fried and sports-bar-friendly. From calamari to wings, from poppers to mozzarella sticks, from freezer to fryer, there's been an evolution of comfort food that American's can't get enough of. Forget cholesterol and calories. Gluten and sodium. Organic and farm-raised. As Pete Kerr of Fry Foods says, "Deep down, it's a sin that isn't hard to forgive."

Recipe

Classic Buffalo Wings

Ingredients

- vegetable oil for frying
- 30 wing segments (flats and drums)
- ⅔ cup Frank's Red Hot sauce (or a preferred brand, but Frank's is traditional)
- 1 cup (2 sticks) unsalted butter
- 2 tbsp. white vinegar
- ½ tsp. Worcestershire sauce
- ¼ tsp. cayenne pepper
- ¼ tsp. garlic powder
- salt to taste

Directions

- Fry wings in 350-degree oil until internal temperature reaches 165 (approximately 12 to 15 minutes), then drain them.

- Combine all remaining ingredients in a saucepan over medium heat. Stir frequently. When sauce comes to a simmer, remove it from heat.

- Place wings in stainless steel bowl, add sauce, and toss until the wings are completely coated.

The All-American Burger

It was perfect for morning television. Photographers in helicopters above, reporters below, wading into the crowd of hundreds of people standing in line for hours. Dozens of drivers lined up in their cars, all waiting for the big event. At times, the lines circled the building at the center of the frenzy three times over. It was a news producer's dream, a spectacle unfolding in real time, all for the opening of a burger joint. White Castle, nearly nonexistent west of the Mississippi, was opening its first outlet in Arizona, near Scottsdale in the Phoenix metro. Finally, the tiny, steamed, pickle-and-onion-adorned White Castle hamburgers known as sliders would be available here. For transplants and snowbirds from back East, locals who'd been introduced to White Castle while traveling, and the simply curious, eager to find out the secret behind the cult favorite that inspired the movie *Harold & Kumar Go to White Castle*, this was a must-attend.

But no one got there before Drew Schmitt and Jamie West, White Castle fanatics who parked their travel trailer in front of the restaurant days ahead of time to claim first place in line. "We got there at nine in the morning, Saturday morning," Jamie says. "So, we camped out for ninety-six hours." And when the big day arrived, she says, "Oh, man, that was an epic morning. We woke up at five and we were too excited to sleep." Drew, big, burly, and bearded, and Jamie, thin and about a foot shorter, dressed in medieval costumes to "storm the castle." She says the experience was "like going to Disneyland." So were the lines, which stretched so long that the wait reached three-and-a-half hours.

"They had no idea that they were going to get slammed as hard as they did," Jamie says. "People were driving in from California, Nevada, Tucson, New Mexico." When the doors finally opened, the crowd went wild. While it's not unusual for customers to order a dozen or more of the chain's small burgers—the company's original slogan was "Buy 'Em by the Sack"—some of the first customers went far beyond that. After several orders for hundreds of sliders each, management imposed a sixty-slider limit. And still, the staff was struggling to keep up. The restaurant is set up to cook 240 burgers at a time—eight grills, each packed with forty sliders, sizzling and steaming and filling the kitchen with the sweet smell of onions—but on this day, that wasn't enough. Extra grills were set up outside under tents. White Castle CEO Lisa Ingram, whose grandfather founded the chain, and Vice President Jamie Richardson, who married into the family, took their turns working the grills, immersed in the sizzles and the smells. "It's a sensory experience," Richardson says. "You've got this melding of beef and bun and onion and pickle." And it was nonstop. "It's exhilarating," he says, "to be able to try to keep up in that environment, it's not easy, but it's worth it." In total, almost fifty-thousand sliders would be sold before management threw up their hands and closed the twenty-four-hour-a-day restaurant for five hours overnight to restock and catch up.

The immense turnout was as much emotional as gustatory. Jessica Pucci, who waited "only" an hour in the drive-through line, says, "I remember going to White Castle with my grandma and grandpa, ordering a big sack of sliders, and loving it." Drew Schmitt says he and Jamie West heard similar stories from the first day they set up their trailer. "Every five to seven minutes somebody else would pull up," he says. "And they would say, 'Hey, did they open yet?' It's like, 'nope.' And we would continue to hear their entire story about where they grew up, why they love White Castle, and this happened over and over and over until like two in the morning, where we finally went to bed. And I think that sums it up. Everyone has a memory of White Castle and it goes back to the childhood memory things of tastes, smells, things like that. And people love them."

In the world of fast-food burgers, White Castle is not one of the big boys. It ranks fifteenth in revenue, outsold many times over by McDonalds, Burger King, Wendy's, and the like. McDonalds revenue is forty billion dollars. White Castle brought in $568 million. Yet, its importance in hamburger history is immense. Says historian Paul Freedman of Yale University, author of *American Cuisine*, "White Castle certainly is responsible for the burger becoming an American icon."

Brought to America in the nineteenth century as Hamburg steak by German immigrants, the hamburger was never high class, but it was cheap. Then, in 1906, it became terrifying after Upton Sinclair's fact-based novel *The Jungle* exposed the shocking dangers to consumers of grievously unsanitary packinghouses that routinely turned out contaminated, adulterated, old, and otherwise inedible meat. White Castle would attack that fear head-on, building a chain of restaurants designed to create a sense of cleanliness and safety.

Designed to look like castles, their buildings were all white on the outside, white porcelain and stainless steel on the inside. Says Historian David Gerard Hogan, author of the definitive history of White Castle, *Selling 'em by the Sack*, "They wanted to show that they were hospital clean, that it was a very clean, sterile environment to get your food." Which was cooked in full view of the customers, visual proof that the meat itself was clean and sanitary.

The creative genius behind this revolutionary idea was Edgar Waldo "Billy" Ingram, a former insurance salesman and real estate agent who opened the first White Castle in 1921 with a partner he would soon buy out. And Ingram didn't just save the burger business, he revolutionized it, inventing the burger chain.

"The standardization is the most important part for them," says hamburger historian George Motz, author of *Hamburger America*. "They standardized the look of the building," he says. "They standardized the buns, the way the beef was ground, the way the beef was eventually pressed. It was actually called the White Castle System because it was all about standardizing everything."

Including the way in which the food was made—one-ounce burgers, which eventually would be standardized as square patties, since that shape allowed more on the grill at once.

From the instant they opened, White Castle was a huge success, inspiring scores of imitators copying their look and even their name. "In the 1920s in America," says Motz, just a touch hyperbolically, "if you didn't put the word 'white' in your hamburger restaurant, you weren't going to sell burgers." There was White Tower, White Fortress, White Diamond, White Rose, White Manna, White Clock, and many more built to resemble the original, with designs emphasizing white tile and stainless steel. "It was a tsunami," says Hogan. "When you see a successful product, a successful company, people are going to try to imitate that success." As they did, the burger was legitimized and popularized, on its way to becoming America's signature food, sold not just at White Castle and its clones, but also at individually owned hamburger stands, mom-and-pop joints, drive-ins, casual restaurants, and diners.

And eventually at a new wave of mega-chains, which would change the game after the Second World War by following Americans from cities to suburbs, and from downtown locations to the exits of the newly created Interstate Highway System. The giant among those, of course, is McDonald's. It was visionary businessman Ray Kroc who saw the potential in the burger restaurant the McDonald brothers created in Riverside, California, with a system that took White Castle's emphasis on standardization even further, breaking burger making into segments, each performed by different people assigned to each station, like an auto assembly line, with a focus on speed, price, and consistency.

In 1962 he bought them out and, through franchising, took their idea nationwide, a business model quickly adopted by their competitors, but not White Castle, which prefers to own all its locations. As a result, there are 362 White Castles in the US today and almost 14,000 McDonald's, more than 7,000 Burger Kings, and nearly 6,000 Wendy's. To this day, McDonald's makes more money from real estate, leasing its locations to franchisees, then it does from actually selling food. McDonald's gargantuan size is almost mind boggling—from Happy Meals alone, it is the world's biggest distributor of toys. With more than 38,000 locations in more than a hundred countries, McDonald's feeds sixty-nine million customers every day. Total sales in 2019 totaled a hundred billion dollars.

And why not? McDonald's and its competitors are fast, convenient, and inexpensive. What they are not is unique or special. And while their food is consistent, it is a far cry from the burgers still to be found at the mom-and-pops, the independent, often family-owned hamburger joints, that have served generations of loyal customers. Places such as the Triple XXX Family Restaurant in West Lafayette, Indiana, opened in 1929 and owned today by Greg and Carrie Ehresman, who took over from Greg's parents in 1999. Carrie says, "We met there. His mom and dad met there. His dad's been coming in since he was four or five. He lived down the street from the restaurant. It's really, truly, in Greg's blood." And many others in the area feel the same way. Alan Karpick, having lunch here with a couple of friends, says, "My relatives, distant relatives, actually ran the Triple XXX in the twenties or thirties." Karpick grew up here, has been coming to the Triple XXX since he was six years old, and ought to be on their payroll as a spokesman. "This is a place I talk up every chance I get," he says. "It's a place that, if you're coming to West Lafayette, whether you're involved with Purdue or just the community itself, it's a place you need to try. It's an institution."

And hard to miss. The exterior is painted in wide strips of brown and blazing orange. There's a walk-up window and a patio for outdoor seating under a metal roof strung with Christmas lights, parking lines still visible on the asphalt from years ago when customers would pull in and order from carhops on roller skates. Inside seating, suspended during the COVID pandemic, is at a horseshoe-shaped counter topped with aging Formica. Decorations include pictures of sports stars from nearby Purdue University and a Purdue-branded sledgehammer in a transparent case. It's all a little shabby in a wonderful way, like an aging fashion model whose smile is now amplified by laugh lines. But the decor isn't the main attraction here. The burgers are. Carrie says, "Our best compliment is somebody that says, 'I haven't been back here in thirty years or forty years,' or, 'I graduated from Purdue and it tastes exactly the way I remember and exactly the way it tasted when I was a student here.' "

Greg says, "The quality is in the cut and how you cook it." He only buys a cut called top-butt sirloin, choice grade. "I can buy cheaper meat all day long. And I can call it exactly the same thing. But what happens is then I'm a liar," he says. "I'm not going to lie to the customer and say, 'Oh my God, it's a steak burger, it's this, it's that,' if it isn't." And beyond the cut, Greg's hamburgers are made entirely by hand. The sirloin is cut into strips and ground onsite. Then it's fed into the Hollymatic-54—it must have seemed like a great name back in 1954 when it was first put on the market—an ancient, dull metal machine sitting on a small stainless steel worktable. Ground beef goes in the top and, amid a cacophony of rattling and shaking, thick patties come out the bottom.

While this happens upstairs, Rodrigo Perez is working the grill in the main restaurant area down below. A little stocky, with close cropped hair, and wearing khaki shorts under his apron, he is making Triple XXX burgers the way they've been made for decades. He grabs a patty, drops it into a metal container filled with flour, coats both sides, slams it on the counter with the heel of his hand four times until it's about half its original one-inch height, then places it on the grill, which has been prepped with canola oil. Then he repeats the process until as many as a dozen patties are lined up and sizzling. After three or four minutes, he flips the burgers, then starts building them according to the row of order slips hanging above him while he starts toasting buns as well. He crisscrosses two strips of bacon on a couple of patties. Drops American cheese on several others. And onions. Pickles. Lettuce. Whatever the customer wants.

More often than any other, the combination Rodrigo ends up building is the burger the Triple XXX is famous for, the Duane Purvis All American, named for a legendary Purdue football player.

"We've met Duane Purvis's son," Carrie says, "and the story he tells and what we've heard is that when they started serving chop steaks, burgers, which we still really do that, he asked to have peanut butter on it, and according to his son, he said, 'My dad put peanut butter on everything, like a slice of bacon, peanut butter sandwich, pancakes, waffles, bananas, apples. If it sat still, my dad put peanut butter on it.' And that's how the peanut butter burger started, in 1932, or something like that."

When it's time to make yet another one, Rodrigo grabs a dented red can from a shelf above the grill and scoops up a glob of Jif peanut butter with a knife that lives inside it. He spreads the peanut butter on the bottom half of a now-toasted bun, puts a cheese-covered burger on top, pickles, and onions on top of that, adds the other half of the bun, and sends another Duane Purvis All American on its way. And he has to keep them coming. Tyler, a Purdue freshman here with his parents during a break from moving into his dorm, is trying his first Duane Purvis. "It's surprisingly better than I thought it would be," he says, "I've never had peanut butter on a burger, but I like it, it's good. I'd definitely order it again or try to make it at home."

Benjamin, a sophomore also here with his parents, says, "The peanut butter actually pairs pretty well. It's an interesting flavor." But it's more than just the peanut butter. "It's super tender," he says, "it's just a solid burger."

And Alan Karpick is having a Duane Purvis, too. The peanut butter makes it unique," he says. It's perfect." And he's got a personal connection to the burger's backstory. "I actually knew Duane Purvis back in the day," he says, "But I also like the sandwich."

It is signature burgers like the Duane Purvis All American that help define mom-and-pop hamburger restaurants all across the country. The deep-fried hamburger at Dyer's in Memphis—they claim they haven't changed the oil in a hundred years but say they do filter it every day. The Juicy Lucy, a burger filled with molten cheese, created at Matt's Bar in Minneapolis and now served at enough other places to have become a so-called regional style, common in a particular state or region, virtually unknown most everywhere else. In fact, the map of America could just as easily be divided by regional burgers as by states. The butter burger in Wisconsin—just as it sounds, a burger topped with a big hunk of butter, sometimes with butter even mixed into the meat; The onion burger in Oklahoma, invented during the depression as a way to save money by mixing onions into the burgers to stretch the beef; The slugburger in Mississippi, also created to save a few cents by mixing flour and other extenders into the meat; The green chile cheeseburger in New Mexico, topped with that state's famous condiment and supposedly enjoyed by scientists working on the first atomic bomb at Los Alamos in 1945; The Carolina burger, topped with chili, Carolina mustard sauce, and coleslaw; Utah's pastrami burger, with a slice of the peppery deli meat atop the patty; The San Antonio bean burger, smothered in Cheez Whiz, refried beans, Fritos and onions; The olive burger in Michigan, topped with olives or an olive and mayo spread; The California burger, with avocado and bacon; The Frita Cubana in South Florida, a burger topped with shoestring fries that was brought here by Cuban immigrants.

Kevin Alexander has tried virtually all of them. In 2017, he sampled 330 burgers in a year for a Thrillist.com article on America's best burgers. "A burger is democratic," he says. "If you really want to understand the city, you should go find the best burger places so you really understand the dynamics of a city, you understand the different neighborhoods by its burgers, and you can also understand, as you get into the regional side of things, you start to understand the history of places." Even if it's tougher to understand the appeal of some of the local favorites. Alexander says, "Connecticut is famous for steamed cheeseburgers and it's like, why do you want a burger that you essentially put in a dishwasher? It doesn't really make sense to me and I don't find them delicious, but that's this strange regional quirk." And he did rank the steamed cheeseburger at Ted's Restaurant in Meriden, Connecticut, number seventy-five on his list of the hundred best burgers in America.

He named "Nick's" cheeseburger with grilled onions at Stanich's, a small Portland restaurant which opened in 1949, as number one. Alexander explains the burger, "was just perfect composition. The onions that had been marinating in something for a long time before they were put on the grill, there was a red pepper relish and some sort of honey mustard built on either side of it." But more than the individual ingredients, it was the way they came together. "There was just this sensory explosion," Alexander says, "and that's what you're looking for. You want to have those 'oh, wow' moments and that just did it for me. It was remarkable, and it was remarkable how in a place as unremarkable as Stanich's to have that sort of experience, which made it even better." But "unremarkable" has always been a hallmark of the best of America's greatest burger joints, everyday places selling an everyday product at a family-friendly price.

Yet these days, burgers have moved far beyond their "unremarkable" roots. They're served at thousands of white tablecloth restaurants throughout the country. In 1985, the Union Square Café, which would set the template for a new generation of restaurants—both relaxed and upscale, serving outstanding food while still remaining trendy—opened in New York with a burger on the menu. In the following years, hip and expensive restaurants in New York and other major cities began offering a burger as well. There had been a hamburger on the menu at New York's tony 21 Club since 1950, but that was a historical oddity and what was happening a half-century later was the beginning of a movement. The most influential burger may be the one Chef Daniel Boulud serves at several of his restaurants. Considered one of the world's greatest chefs and a major influence throughout the culinary world, Boulud presides over an international empire of elite restaurants from New York to Dubai, including his flagship, the two-Michelin-starred Daniel in Manhattan. Says George Motz, "If Daniel Boulud is going to put a hamburger on the menu, it's going to be a high-end burger. It's going to be a crazy thing. That's exactly what it was. It became one of the famous hamburgers in history."

Boulud says he got the idea in part back in the year 2000, when a reporter from the *New York Times* asked him about an anti-McDonald's protest in France. "The journalist interviewed me," he says, "and I was joking saying, 'I guess maybe they are jealous that the Americans created the burger in the first place and it wasn't the French, and that's why maybe they burned down McDonald's.' " But jokes aside, Boulud says he was intrigued by the idea of making a hamburger the French way. "I want to create a gourmet burger. I want to create a burger where you open a very good bottle of wine." So, he went to work. "I combine the most iconic dish in America, which is burger, with the most iconic and successful dish on my menu [at Daniel] which was the braised short ribs in red wine," he says, "and by combining those two together, I basically created a monster." In some ways, Boulud invented an upscale Juicy Lucy, a burger stuffed not with cheese, but with a hunk of shredded short ribs, which in turn is stuffed with a slice of foie gras and surrounded by frisée, tomato compote, fresh tomato, raw onion, French mustard, mayonnaise, and grated horseradish, all on a buttered, pan-toasted, brioche-like potato bun that's topped with poppy seeds, cracked pepper, and shredded parmesan. When the burger is cut in half, each element is revealed like the rings of a redwood or the interior of a turducken. When it was first sold in 2001, when a McDonalds burger cost seventy-nine cents, Boulud's cost twenty-nine dollars.

The *Guinness Book of World Records* declared it the most expensive burger in the world. This led other restaurateurs to chase that title, marketing burgers that cost a hundred dollars or more. Chef Hubert Keller recently put a burger on the menu at his restaurant in Las Vegas with a price tag of five thousand dollars. The burger, made with wagyu beef, foie gras, and truffles, came with a bottle of 1995 Chateau Petrus, one of the most expensive wines on earth, and still the price tag far exceeded the sum of the parts.

But beyond his gimmicky imitators, Boulud unleased the white tablecloth burger, legitimizing countless upscale incarnations of the American classic. "I gave the opportunity for so many chefs to express themselves through the burger," Boulud says. "And I think that's something to be proud of."

But how to do it? After all, whatever the price, whatever the setting, at heart, a burger is still some version of ground beef on a bun. Often, the answer is unusual toppings. Often, it is size. Or sides. Or some special house-made bun. And then there's the special blend, a concept invented by New York area meat supplier Pat LaFrieda, who's become a celebrity in the food world as a result. "I wanted to appeal to more restaurants," LaFrieda says, "and I knew that in order to do so, we could not sell everyone the same blend, and different restaurants, especially in New York City, [where there are] three or four restaurants on one street, they needed to have different experiences depending on what that chef wanted. And that's how we became known for our burger blends." LaFrieda says each blend is a different combination of cuts, fat percentage, and grind, giving each restaurant a burger available nowhere else, unique in both taste and texture.

He now makes a specific blend for each of 350 different commercial customers. That's 350 different restaurants (stand-alone, concept, or chain), each offering consumers something unique and often making a point of it right on the menu. The Minetta Tavern in New York, for example, named its thirty-three-dollar Black Label Burger for the LaFrieda blend it's made of. There's even special-blend fast food. Shake Shack uses a LaFrieda blend and describes the burgers that result as "100 percent Angus beef that's humanely raised, vegetarian fed, and source verified" and "made from premium whole muscle cuts—with no hormones or antibiotics, ever."

A far cry from "You deserve a break today," it's the kind of story being told by a growing number of so-called "better burger" chains. Like Shake Shack, some tout the natural or organic pedigree of their beef. Others simply promise handmade, high-quality burgers cooked to order. Smashburger, for example. And Better Burger market leader Five Guys, which boasts of making great burgers out of fresh, never frozen, high-quality beef that is 80 percent lean and 20 percent fat. "We just wanted to have a hamburger that was like a mom and pop," says CEO Jerry Murrell, who founded the company with his sons in 1986. From the beginning, he says, that meant paying for quality ingredients. "The kids knew this guy that sold meat to high-end restaurants, Steve the meat man," he says. "They went to him and said, 'Hey, can you get us hamburger?' And he said, 'Yeah.' Of course, his prices were high, and everybody said we should by from Cisco and all that. But we said, 'No, we'll buy it from this guy.' "

Thirty-seven years later, commanding half of the "better burger" market and having expanded from one restaurant to 1,600, a growing number of them in other countries, Five Guys has moved on to higher volume meat suppliers. But Murrell insists the quality is still the same. The burgers are even pattied by hand, the ground beef first formed into a meatball, then flattened with a hand-held metal press. The burgers, just over three-and-a-half ounces each, are cooked on a flattop, mashed down with a spatula just once before being flipped. And the standard burger on the menu is a stack of two patties, though a single is available. Since the number of toppings is left to the customer, the final product is often beautifully messy, condiments poking out everywhere, melted cheese running down the sides. Surprisingly, given how beloved the burgers are, Five Guys will not serve them red or even pink on the inside. Only well done.

And every burger at Five Guys—and virtually every other better burger chain—is made to order, nothing held under a heat lamp. Food scientists say the longer a burger is held, the more its flavor and texture can chemically degrade. But there's one other claim central to every better burger chain that may not be as important as it seems, the use of fresh beef, never frozen, especially when the burger is topped with condiments. "The likelihood is that there are subtle differences between fresh and frozen," says meat scientist Dr. Chris Calkins, "but to be honest with you, by the time you get it on a bun, and you make your burger, that difference is usually nondetectable." So, does it matter? Jerry Murrell says, "It doesn't to most people. But to me it does and to my kids it does." And clearly to enough consumers that McDonald's is now selling quarter pounders made with fresh beef, not frozen. At some locations, White Castle is selling a fresh beef burger called the 1921 burger, in honor of the year the company was founded. Burger King, which tested fresh beef Whoppers but has not made the switch from frozen, is taking a different path, offering a Whopper with no beef at all.

The Impossible Whopper uses a patty made entirely from plants, created by Impossible Foods. Unlike previous veggie-burgers, it is supposed to mimic the taste, look, and feel of beef, even "bleeding" when cut or bitten into. Similar products have been added to the menus at a variety of other chains, including White Castle, and the co-owned Carl's Jr. and Hardees. But will they make a significant dent in the sale of traditional hamburgers? Expert opinions are split, and food industry analyst David Palmer says franchisees are not excited to have them on the menu. "They don't seem to believe it's a huge idea," he says. "What has been a modest success at Burger King, our sense is that it will have a modest following and a carve-out demand of a few percent of all burgers. But likely not much greater than that." BurgerFi and Elevation Burger do sell plant-based burgers and some of the other better burger chains do have vegetarian options, but their impact on total sales has not been great. The biggest change for hamburger chains, in fact, has been the increasing popularity of chicken on their menus, generally sandwiches and pieces called strips, tenders, nuggets, and such.

It is the beef hamburger that remains the quintessential American food just as it has been for a very long time. CEO Tony Darden of the MOOYAH "better burger" chain says, "There is a nostalgia of just the feeling you get when you have a burger, because it takes you back to these memories or these things you think about where you are enjoying time with your family and friends." George Motz says, "The bottom line is people want the burger they remember."

Such as the burger—and the experience—at Louis' Lunch in New Haven, Connecticut, a small brick building with bright red shutters and door, on the corner of Crown Street and Sherman's alley in the shadow of Yale University. The interior is reminiscent of an old English pub—dark, with diamond-shaped panes in two arch-topped windows, exposed brick walls, wooden beams and tables, and a long wooden pew with extended arms like the writing surface on an old elementary school desk, with names and initials carved into the wood everywhere. Behind a long counter, there's a narrow, cramped cooking area, where a staff of three dances a continuing ballet to avoid collisions while taking and tending to orders. Louis' Lunch claims to have created the first "hamburger sandwich." It's an ultimately unprovable assertion—there are a variety of other contenders—but it's irrefutable that founder Louis Lassen began serving burgers in 1900.

His great-grandson and current Louis' Lunch owner Jeff Lassen tells the story. "A customer came in and was in a great rush and said, 'I've got to get the heck out of here. What can you do to help me out?' And he thought for a moment, he said, 'You know, if I chop this [steak] up, put it between two slices of bread, so then I can send him on his way and make him happy, hopefully.' And that's all she wrote." Lassen says his great-grandfather cooked that original burger in one of the gas-fired broilers he had been using for steaks, and they are still in used today. "The date is just cast in the side of each one, 1898, so they're 122 years old," he says, "and they cook vertically and there's a flame on either side with two small doors that open. And we insert a rack and you cook on the rack inside the broilers and you can cook as many as nine at a time."

The options are limited here. The only available toppings are American cheese, tomato, and onion. No ketchup. No mustard. Not even a slice of pickle. And there are no buns either—every burger is served on white toast, which some purists say removes Louis' Lunch from the first-burger competition, since true burgers require buns, but passions run just as high on the other side of the debate.

These days, Louis' Lunch gets a substantial tourist trade from all over the world. But at heart, this historic icon is a local joint with a crowd of devoted regulars, like so many family-owned burger restaurants all across the country. Lassen says, "We have bank presidents and custodians to teachers, to healthcare workers, to scientists, to you name it." And many have been coming for decades. "We're fortunate in that," he says. "When you form friendships over the years with families and they bring their kids and then they bring their kids and they bring their kids. So, there's three and four generations of families eating there at some times." Lassen says, "It goes back so far and so long, and people have been enjoying it for so long and sharing it with family members." A perfect reflection of the place the hamburger holds in the cultural history of the country. "It's just become part of our heritage and part of Americana."

Triple XXX Duane Purvis All American Burger

Ingredients

- 4 oz. coarsely ground 80 percent lean sirloin (top sirloin butt if available)
- 4.5-inch sesame seed bun
- dusting of flour
- drizzle of vegetable oil
- 1 slice American cheese
- 1 tbsp. creamy peanut butter
- 4 dill pickle slices
- 1 slice onion, cut thin
- 1 iceberg lettuce leaf
- 1 slice tomato

Directions

- Toast the bun. Form the ground beef into a loose patty, dip both sides in flour, then press the patty until it is 4.5 to 5 inches in diameter. Spread a small amount of oil on the patty with a pastry brush. Place the patty in a heated, oiled cast iron skillet. When the flour is almost dissipated, flip the patty and cook to preference.

- Top with American cheese and remove it from the skillet when the cheese melts. Spread peanut butter on the bottom bun while the bun is warm. Place the patty on top of the peanut butter. Top the patty with pickle slices, onion, lettuce, and tomato. Add the top bun.

Made in America— Our Love Affair with Chinese Food

The young woman behind the counter is explaining my options, pointing to the dozen or more stainless-steel containers laid out in front of her, and explaining what's in them. I, of course, understand nothing as she is speaking Mandarin and I don't. Mia, a friend of a friend is translating for me and making suggestions. So is her fiancé, Ryan. They are helping me decide what I want in my "dry pot," a stir-fried assortment of whatever a customer chooses, priced by weight. I go with beef, fish, tofu skin, crab, seaweed, tripe, and kidney. I pass on the artery.

One stall over, a man dressed all in white is pounding a big hunk of dough, preparing to hand-pull fresh noodles to serve in soup. We order two bowls, one with lamb, the other with beef tendon. A few stands down the line, we order duck soup, and nearby we watch a woman expertly ladling crepe dough onto a hot circular cooking surface, just as they do in France. Unlike in France though, two of the finished crepes are layered with fillings in between, then folded and tucked, almost like a rectangular burrito. We order two.

And we've only scratched the surface. We are in a massive food court, dozens of booths offering all manner of Chinese favorites— fish balls, sausages, steamed buns, potato noodles, dumplings, sliced fish in hot chili oil, and much, much more, all cooked fresh right in front of you. Prices are low—seven dollars, eight, nothing more than ten. The place is packed, at least two hundred people at row after row of rectangular tables. As we wind our way to the seats other friends have claimed and held for us, we pass three young women sharing skewers of meat and a big wooden bowl full of crab and vegetables, one table over from four older men deep in conversation while hunched over their noodles. There are young couples. Older couples. Singles. Parents with young children, many pushing strollers.

The dishes we pile on our table represent a variety of regions in China, which boasts a culinary tradition stretching back five-thousand years, a cuisine that emphasizes not just a variety of flavors, but also of textures. The beef tendon in our noodle and soup bowl has a deep, rich taste, chewy but with a jelly-like texture. The lamb, tender, nice flavor, not too gamey. In the blindingly spicy dry pot, kidney—something I had previously avoided—is surprisingly good, reminiscent of liver but a little softer. And the fish, to my surprise, is lightly battered and fabulous. The overriding flavor is a searing spiciness (which I learn had been toned down for me when Mia placed our order).

The duck soup is wonderfully rich. The gizzard in it is a bit tough for my taste, but the slice of congealed duck blood served on the side, while unfortunately honestly named, has a uniquely bright flavor and a texture similar to liverwurst. The pancakes, savory and spicy, combine two textures—the outer dough is soft, but a crunchy piece of fried dough is hidden inside. It is terrific and Ryan agrees, telling me, "This has been my breakfast in all my four years of college." That was in Shanghai, where he'd buy them from a food truck outside his dorm.

But we are not in Shanghai. Or in China at all on this October day in 2019. We are in Flushing, a neighborhood in the New York City borough of Queens. And yes, this is a food court, but not in the American fast-food way. Here, everything is fresh and cooked in front of you when you order it. Seemingly everyone is speaking some dialect of Chinese. Fueled by growing immigration, Flushing is now home to thousands of Chinese immigrants, many of them graduate students and professionals, who have grown up in a changing China, with a fast-growing economy, an expanding middle class, and much wider ability to travel. The food here is intended for them. It's what they ate back home—or at least as close as possible, given the availability of necessary ingredients. It's not the Chinese American dishes developed decades ago to please the American palate, the dishes I grew up loving, like General Tso's chicken and beef with broccoli.

Fuchsia Dunlop, writer, cookbook author, winner of four James Beard awards, and an acclaimed expert on Chinese food says, "There are a whole lot more Chinese students and immigrants who are not just the chefs, but the market for the Chinese restaurants. So Chinese restaurants these days do not need to adapt to mainstream American Western tastes. They can open in areas like San Gabriel Valley, [California, and in Flushing] really designed to satisfy Chinese people. And so that's why there's this kind of really authentic regional cuisine."

And beyond that, as we will soon see, there is a new generation of highly trained chefs fighting for Chinese cooking to finally get the respect it deserves, evolving Chinese food in America, pushing boundaries, attempting to elevate it to the same status as high-end French or Japanese cuisine, with prices to match. That, after decades of Americans embracing the Chinese food they've seemingly always known as familiar, plentiful, and cheap, a formula that has been astoundingly successful.

There are more Chinese restaurants in America than all the McDonald's, Burger Kings, Wendy's, and KFCs combined, at last count, more than fifty thousand. Almost all serving a familiar roster of dishes created by Chinese immigrants as much as two centuries ago. Dishes never seen in China, made specifically to please the American palate. And they nailed it, making Chinese American food—from beef and broccoli to General Tso's chicken, from egg rolls to spareribs—an American staple.

So how did we get here? It all began with gold. The California Gold Rush attracted thousands of Chinese men hoping to strike it rich, and hundreds who set up stores and restaurants to keep them supplied and fed. Soon, non-Chinese miners began dining at those restaurants, which were identifiable by triangular yellow flags out front and offered big portions at low prices. The miners sometimes ordered American dishes the Chinese cooks had figured out how to make, but many ate what the Chinese ate. And they liked it. Miner William Shaw reported in 1851, "The best eating houses in Francisco are those kept by the Celestials, and conducted in a Chinese fashion; the dishes are mostly curries, hashes and fricassees, served in small dishes and as they were exceedingly palatable, I was not curious enough to inquire about the ingredients."

Despite widespread racism, the Chinese were tolerated, if not welcome, until the gold began to run out. Then they were seen as a threat to American jobs. Politicians called for their expulsion and passed laws barring them from many occupations. Violence broke out against them—shootings, lynchings, mob attacks.

Many Chinese were killed, and entire communities were burned to the ground. By the 1870s and 1880s, thousands had fled California. Those who did not return to China headed east, creating Chinatowns in communities all across the country along with unemployed Chinese workers who had been building the now-completed transcontinental railroad.

But they could not escape the racism. It may have been less violent, but it was everywhere, the Chinese mercilessly disparaged by politicians and the media as dirty and primitive, accused of eating rats. Chinatowns were depicted as dangerous havens of sin, rife with opium and prostitution, where women were supposedly at risk of being abducted into so-called "white slavery."

Yet for some Americans, that made a trip to Chinatown an irresistible adventure, most notably in New York beginning in the 1880s. Culinary historian Andrew Coe, author of *Chop Suey: A Cultural History of Chinese Food in the United States*, explains, "The people who first discovered Chinese food as a thing that is good were the Bohemians. And they were like the artist, theatrical crowd. They were like the cool people who stayed up late. They were the hipsters of their era. And so, they gave these Chinese restaurants a certain kind of cachet. This was like a hip place to hang out." And they would soon be followed by a much wider slice of society. The *Washington Times* reported in 1903, "In Washington there is hardly a night that the Chinese restaurants are not patronized at some hour of the night by fashionably dressed women with escorts in evening attire."

At the other end of the social scale, Chinese restaurants offered a refuge for minorities unwelcome elsewhere. Jews and African Americans. Paradoxically, for the families of Jewish immigrants, eating Chinese food was seen as a big step toward fitting in. Sociologist Gaye Tuchman, coauthor of a seminal academic study on Jews and Chinese food, says it made them feel cosmopolitan: "It was a certain experience as part of a social strata. So, what we're talking about when we say it made you feel cosmopolitan is, it made you feel American."

And food that wasn't kosher, such as pork and shellfish, somehow seemed easier to justify when it was diced and hidden among vegetables and sauce. In Yiddish, non-Kosher food is said to be "treyf," meaning unclean. What Jews ate in Chinatown would come to be called "safe treyf." And, like the Bohemians, one of their favorites was something called chop suey, a combination of stir-fried vegetables and some kind of protein, all covered in a thick brown sauce.

Some culinary historians claim chop suey was a fraud, a dish passed off to unsuspecting Americans as Chinese even though it was invented here out of whole cloth, just exotic enough, with bamboo shoots and water chestnuts, to seem exciting, but with texture and gravy reminiscent of popular American stews. Others insist it is a modification of a dish made in China, where it featured entrails and offal among the vegetables, instead of the beef, pork, or chicken in the Americanized version. What is certain is that chop suey ignited America's love affair with Chinese food. And the turning point was one event, an official visit to the United States in 1896 by a senior Chinese government official, Li Hongzhang.

The public was transfixed by this visitor from afar. The newspapers went wild with coverage. What he did. How he dressed. What he ate, which according to several newspapers and wire services featured chop suey. In reality, there is no evidence that he ever even tasted the dish; it seems certain, in fact, that he did not. But that didn't matter a bit. The newspapers said he did, and suddenly eating chop suey was seen as sophisticated and exciting. Restaurant signs began featuring the words "chop suey," often more prominently than the names of the restaurants themselves. The *New York Times* declared in 1900, "The city has gone 'chop-suey' mad." By 1924, there were more than 250 Chinese restaurants in New York alone, many of them outside of Chinatown.

The craze took hold in San Francisco, Chicago, St. Louis, Atlanta, pretty much everywhere. Coe says, "When the chop suey boom started, and particularly after about 1898, that's when there was a real impetus for Americans all over the country to try chop suey and these restaurants and they saw that there was a market all over the place. And that's when the restaurants began to start opening up. And by the 1920s, there was a Chinese restaurant in just about every city and every large town in the United States."

Including Butte, Montana, where the Pekin Noodle Parlor opened in 1911 and still proudly features chop suey, sixty or seventy years after it disappeared from so many Chinese restaurant menus, victim of changing tastes and questions about its origins. Jerry Tam is the fifth generation of his family to run the Pekin, which he claims is the oldest Chinese restaurant in America. "It's a one of a kind, one of the most special places on earth." he says.

And he is proudly looking backward. "We are truly an original chop suey house," he says. The neon sign jutting out from the second story of the weathered brick building stacks big red letters from top to bottom to spell out "chop suey." The menu lists fourteen different kinds of chop suey—pork, chicken, shrimp, almond, and more. Tam says, "It is a combination of whatever's left over in vegetables, onions, greens, celery, bean sprouts. And you could put bok choy in it, you can put anything you want in it. It's just tiny bits of vegetables all mixed together and prepared in its own vegetable gravy."

Big batches are made several times a night—vegetables chopped on one thick cutting board, meats on another, all stir-fried in sizzling woks that have been tarnished by decades of use, one so old it's almost totally black. Ladle the chop suey onto a pile of crispy noodles and it becomes chow mein. The rest of the menu is made up of Chinese American classics, most of which developed in the years, even decades, after chop suey took the country by storm and restaurateurs responded by creating more dishes, many of them sweet or crunchy, to appeal to American tastes. The Pekin Noodle Parlor menu lists sweet and sour pork and chicken, eight varieties of fried rice, spareribs, won tons, egg foo young. And combination specials, like one Tam describes as "fried rice, chop suey, sweet and sour chicken, fried wontons, noodles, barbecued pork, everything good that we do. It just really makes people happy."

Everything here is made fresh. In the kitchen, one woman is filling and rolling eggrolls, another, hunched over making won tons, while one cook spends the night making the sweet and sour dishes, dipping each piece into a sticky white batter, lowering them into the deep fryer and back up, steaming, crunchy, and ready to be sauced. Tam says his favorite is crispy, deep-fried sweet and sour pork rib. Affection for the restaurant runs deep, with succeeding generations of local families returning year after year. Tam says, "When you treat them with kindness and you give them good cooked food, it's great."

This evening, the Johnson family, pleasantly boisterous and laughing, has commandeered a large table near the front of the narrow second-floor dining room. Shar and Dale Johnson have been coming here since they were high school sweethearts in the sixties. They're surrounded by family members from the next three generations, right down to great-grandson Hudson, an active baby boy, whose mother, Jordan declares flatly, "This is the best Chinese food you will ever have. I know it sounds weird; it's in Butte, Montana. But trust me, you won't have better."

Tam says of course people come for the food, but he says there's much more, the sense of walking into a different world. "It's foreign food and it's in the setting," he says. "It's the color scheme. There's still red everywhere, yellow. It's a complete different culture, feels comfortable." Comfortably exotic. For decades, the Chinese restaurant template would remain unchanged—decor heavy on pagodas, lanterns, and dragons. And a virtually identical menu of "Chinese food," Americanized descendants of Cantonese food, since Canton was where the Gold Rush immigrants had come from, even though cuisine in China has historically been regional, not national.

Cecilia Chiang, a towering figure in the development of Chinese cuisine in America, who tutored Julia Child, Alice Waters, and James Beard, told me just ten months before she passed away at a hundred years of age, "In China we have so many good foods, such a big country. Each province has their own way of cooking." This is increasingly represented these days on even everyday Chinese restaurant menus in America, to a great extent because of Madame Chiang's determination. "I wanted totally different," she said. "Anything they served [in Chinatown], I don't want in my menu. I want really to introduce the real Chinese food to Americans." The restaurant she opened in San Francisco in 1961, the Mandarin, was elegant and sophisticated. No red and gold decor. No dragons or lanterns. And the menu was based on the kind of food a staff cook would prepare for Madame Chiang's affluent family back in China. "I have very good memory," she said, "and I have a very good palate. I know the food. I grew up with good food."

Energetic and impeccably dressed in black and grey when we met at her tastefully decorated Pacific Heights apartment, she was justifiably proud of her accomplishments. "I have the original menu," she said, "three hundred items, all in Chinese." She slipped it out of a large envelope and showed it to me. There were handwritten revisions in blue pen. Some dishes were scratched out entirely. And almost every dish was unlike anything non-Chinese Americans had seen—or tasted—before. "I had the pot stickers in 1960," she said, "I started chicken baked in clay, beggar's chicken, smoked tea duck, Peking duck. And our famous squab. Then I also started to serve Sichuan food. That time people don't even [know] what does Sichuan mean? What is Sichuan? Now, of course, everybody knows."

In fact, Sichuan cuisine would soon become all the rage, along with other regional Chinese specialties, after a century-old ban on Chinese immigration was relaxed in 1965. Among the wave of new immigrants were some remarkable chefs, bringing some of China's finest dishes. Beijing specialties such as moo shu pork. Shanghai favorites such as red braised pork belly. And from the Sichuan region, spicy dishes such as chicken in hoisin sauce and shrimp in Sichuan sauce. Even hotter dishes from the Hunan region would arrive a short time later.

Then, in 1972, President Richard Nixon and Chinese Premier Mao Zedong met in Beijing, and millions of people watched on television as America's president, using chopsticks, ate a nine course Chinese meal. The spectacle spurred a virtual Chinese food hysteria back home. Author and Food historian Andrew Coe says, "Chop suey and chow mein joints stopped serving so much chow mein and chop suey and started serving kung pao chicken and Sichuan food and Hunan food. And that really changed the way Americans see [Chinese cooking]."

The timing was perfect. Americans were becoming more culinarily adventurous and tastemakers were now on the hunt for what they called "authentic" Chinese cooking, even if, unknown to them, many of the new dishes were being toned down and Americanized. Originally, General Tso's chicken was created in Taiwan as a Hunan dish, tangy and spicy chicken pieces on the bone, but by the time it was popularized at New York's legendary Shun Lee Dynasty, it had been transformed—sticky sweet and boneless. Today, it remains one of the most popular Chinese American dishes ever served, even as menus continue to evolve for a variety of reasons.

For one thing, there has been a changing of the guard. As Cantonese-descended owners retired and their children chose other careers, many were replaced by immigrants from elsewhere in China, mostly from the Fujian province. Overwhelmingly, they left in place the menus they inherited, but increasingly they've been adding some of their own regional cuisine, items such as fish balls and hand-pulled noodles. And even more adventurous dishes are showing up in mid-America as well.

Chef Christine Lau, who has consulted for Chinese restaurants in the Midwest, says, "It happens in pockets," specifically in college towns. "There's a lot of immigrants. There's a market for it." At the Longfei Restaurant in Bloomington, Indiana, across the street from the University of Indiana, owner Xiao Fei Zhou says, "I have authentic Chinese food and I have American Chinese food; I have both of them." His menu has a separate section for each. The so-called authentic dishes include sautéed pig intestines, spicy beef tendon, and sliced pig ear with spicy sauce. The American/Chinese section includes orange chicken, crab Rangoon, shrimp with lobster sauce, and General Tso's chicken.

Zhou, who came to America from Shanghai when he was fifteen, says the "authentic" section is aimed at the many Chinese students attending nearby Indiana University, though they are not the only customers making that choice. "There are lots of American people that like authentic Chinese food," he says. "So, I just say in case they don't like it, they have a chance to order American Chinese food. Everybody that walks in the door won't be disappointed. They'll always find something they like." Some Chinese chefs predict—or hope—that more restaurants in mid-America will follow Longfei's example, adding regional Chinese dishes to their menus. Others are not so optimistic. Still, there is clearly a renaissance underway right now in Chinese cooking, even if it is mostly on the coasts.

It's being called Chinese 2.0, innovative young chefs breaking new ground in a variety of ways. Some replicating traditional Chinese cuisines most Americans don't know. Others using the food they grew up with as inspiration to evolve Chinese food in America, combining traditional tastes and techniques with American ingredients in novel new ways, attempting to broaden the definition and presentation of Chinese food. And they are fighting to bring Chinese food the respect they believe it deserves, to convince American diners it's worth more than takeout prices, in often trendy restaurants that don't conform to the traditional Chinese American aesthetic.

One of the pioneers of Chinese 2.0 is Ning (Amelie) Kang, who came to the United States from China at the age of eighteen and went on to graduate from the Culinary Institute of America. Her two MáLà Project restaurants in New York project a hip, stylish, downtown vibe—exposed brick walls, soft lighting, wood plank benches, communal tables—and recipes straight from China. "When we started at MáLà Project," Kang says, "we just wanted to serve the same kind of food that we would have in China. So, we weren't really looking at what's available here. We just wanted to make uncompromised and the most original foods in the form of dry pot, which is what we specialize in." That's the spicy mix-and-match stir fry I first encountered in Flushing, a dish Kang first tried when she moved to Beijing for high school. With offal for those who wish— tendon, tongue, tripe, stomach, artery and more—but also beef tenderloin, short ribs, fish, prawns, lobster balls, even Spam, all of which Kang says would be on the menu at a dry pot restaurant in Beijing.

And she says food in China isn't locked into yesterday's recipes, especially with increasing personal income and the proliferation of social media. "It changes all the time," she says. "And we have innovation, like even new dishes creations all the time, like dry pot. Dry pot didn't exist until the seventies and now it's everywhere. We have these hot pot skewers that didn't exist when I was younger, so our food changes all the time."

And many of the new chefs aren't striving for the so-called authenticity of perfectly replicating dishes as eaten in China. They're focusing on the soul of Chinese cooking, the flavors and techniques, often done in new ways. Chris Cheung of New York's East Wind Snack Shop says he likes to riff on the classics: "What I'm specifically doing is drawing back from my childhood memories of what Chinese food meant to me and made me happy and all those tastes and flavors, and the picture that I'm trying to create and the image I'm trying to portray is from that."

Cheung remembers growing up in New York's Chinatown, eating in Chinese restaurants, but not necessarily what the tourists were being served. "You had the stuff that was the traditional, authentic stuff that was only written in Chinese on the menu but really wasn't made accessible to an American crowd," he says, "but those restaurants also served General Tso's chicken and beef and broccoli and egg foo yung and chicken chow mein. So, they had both kinds of food and I was aware of both styles and I am nostalgic to that."

He does his own take on beef and broccoli, braising short ribs and putting abalone in the oyster sauce. And fills dumplings with twenty-eight day dry-aged beef. He does his own version of General Tso's chicken. And of a traditional pork bun called a gua bao. He says Chinese food is in the midst of a renaissance. "I think it's definitely evolving. You have two sides," he says, "You have the people who are steeped in tradition and don't want to veer from that, and I love that, I love that, you need that. You need that as a point of history to grow from. And then you also have your envelope pushers who kind of want to see what they can do with the food and see where Chinese food can go and how far it can go and how you can push it with different ingredients and different techniques. I kind of like to be the bridge with kind of one foot in tradition and the other foot at least pointing toward a little bit of a visionary direction. I don't veer too far but I do appreciate it. And it doesn't always work, but I do love when chefs make the effort and without trial and error, they can't be a success."

Tommy Lee knows all about trial and error. At his Hop Alley restaurant in Denver's trendy RiNo (river north) neighborhood, he says he is serving a young, hip clientele that is generally not as culinarily adventurous as many diners in New York or Los Angeles. "We're trying to please our audience without necessarily compromising too much," he says. "We get it now. On our first menu, people were like, 'What is this?' " He says he modifies dishes as needed, but only to a degree. "Most of my approach is like, let's keep the profile of the dish, or at least the flavor profile of the dish, traditional, and let's tweak the elements to maybe make it a little more marketable," he says. "That's why I have no issue taking things off of people's bill because when someone says they don't like something, we say, 'Sorry, that's what the dish is, if you don't like it then we'll take it off your bill, it's no big deal. But that's what the dish is.' "

The new breed of chefs say they are fighting to get Chinese food the respect it deserves as a great cuisine. "I do think that Chinese food gets the short end of the stick," says chef and consultant Christine Lau. "It's that cheap food. You've got your takeout place. Come on, it costs five bucks for lunch, like whatever. It definitely exists across the country."

Taiwan-born George Chen, who has opened fifteen restaurants, including several in China, over the past twenty-five years, says, "I think most Americans think of Chinese food as what they thought of Italian food as, pizza and checkerboard tablecloths and spaghetti and meatballs twenty years ago. Italian food has evolved, Japanese food has come into vogue, high-end sushi restaurants are revered by Michelin and able to charge very steep prices. Chinese food has not gotten that kind of lift, if you will. Most people in America still think of Chinese food as coming in this white box with a mystery brown sauce. It's a stereotype of a great cuisine. And Chinese American food, I don't knock it, I think there's wonderful Chinese American food. But that's not real Chinese food. It's really my major agenda, if you want to call it that, our mission, to change that perception and elevate Chinese food to its proper order."

He has opened China Live, a massive Chinese restaurant and marketplace in San Francisco and, above it in the same building, another restaurant he named Eight Tables. Actually, it has nine, including a chef's table in the kitchen, but eight is a lucky number in China. Here, Chen presents his evolution of Chinese food as haute cuisine. "My cooking is based on the many decades, if not centuries, of Chinese cuisine," he says. "The interpretation of classic techniques with the deep study of the cultural relevance, and then putting a San Francisco George Chen interpretation on it."

And it is a singular experience, as my wife Roberta and I learn one crisp December evening after the chef invites us to dine there. We pass through a chain link fence, down a narrow, dimly-lit alley reminiscent of the back streets of Hong Kong or Shanghai, up an elevator, and into a muted and elegant space—hushed, warm, with light wood and soft lighting—where we are immediately offered hot towels before being led to our round banquette table. This is Chen's homage to a kind of dining in China called Si Fang Cai, extravagant meals prepared by professional chefs in private homes, as he explains: "Si Fang Cai is literally, 'si' is private, 'fang' is house or chateau or estate, and 'cai' is cuisine. So, Si Fang Cai."

It dates back to the Ming Dynasty, which lasted from the fourteenth to the seventeenth century but, as Chen explains, in the last ten or fifteen years it has been resurrected, initially among the monied elites in Taiwan, Hong Kong, and mainland China, where the booming economy has created a new class, the ultra-rich. "They were so rich that they wanted something different," he says. And something discrete: "When Xi Jinping came into power, it was looked down upon to flaunt your wealth. So, they went indoors to these private homes and chateaus to have these meals. And literally, Si Fang Cai became the rage. It just got revitalized in popularity because, when you have money, people want exclusive experiences."

At Eight Tables, that means a ten-course tasting menu for two, with wine or cocktails and other extras, can cost more than a thousand dollars. Most of the dishes have never been seen elsewhere, but Chen says they are all firmly rooted in the past: "Some people say it's like 'Wow, geez, I've had these flavors before when I was growing up. My grandma made a dish that had these flavors and you've elevated it and I'm so happy.' And some even will get emotional."

Our meal begins with a plate of nine morsels, not much more than a bite each, laid out in three rows and described by our waiter as the nine essential flavors of Chinese cuisine, which he lists as sweet, salty, sour, bitter, numbing, spicy, fragrant, fresh, and smoky. The next nine courses, explained as they are served, include an open dumpling shell colored red with beet juice and filled with dabs of shrimp purée topped with caviar, trout roe, scallop mousse and uni; caviar on duck skin with suckling pig and Spanish Iberico ham; poached lobster in a sizzling rice soup; Sichuan black cod with fermented rice porridge and scallion foam;

and many more extravagant creations that I had never seen in any Chinese restaurant before. The range of flavors and textures was extraordinary, as were the preparation and presentation.

This is not the food anyone grew up with in China, the dishes some would call authentic. Chen says he is channeling the essence of a great cuisine, not trying to replicate specific dishes. "Authentic is a terrible word for me," he says. "I think it should be interpreted as cooking with integrity and cooking with a cultural perspective, understanding the basis of how the dish came about. It's not meant to be authentic to anybody. It's based on something that I studied, something that I tasted, something that I have that has inherent basis in the dominion of Chinese cuisine. And I'm proud of the fact that I'm able to do that. What food is not interpretive, what cuisine is not interpretive?"

The mainstream future of Chinese food in America certainly doesn't rest on thousand-dollar meals. But dinner at Eight Tables is just one very extreme example of how far the growing Chinese food revolution in America has come. This is not to suggest that thousands of restaurants serving General Tso's chicken and beef with broccoli are going away any time soon. They represent a beloved American cuisine even adventurous new chefs will tell you is delicious. More are now closing than opening as owners retire and their children choose other less taxing and more economically rewarding professions, but America's love of Chinese food is as strong as ever. There are simply more choices now. From food courts, to hand-pulled noodle shops, to a new breed of restaurants run by creative young chefs, to wallet-busting tasting menus, Chinese food in America is increasingly gaining the long overdue respect it deserves. And if you're ever in Butte, Montana, don't miss the chop suey.

Recipe

Short Rib Wontons

By East Wind Snack Shop Owner Chris Cheung

Ingredient Group One

- 2 pounds beef short rib on the bone
- 2 cups Shao Shing Chinese wine
- 1 tbsp. black peppercorns
- ½ tbsp. cumin seed
- ½ tbsp. coriander seed
- 1 piece of star anise
- 2 cloves garlic
- 2 tbsp. sugar
- ½ cup soy sauce
- ¼ cup vegetable oil
- approximately 1 pint of water
- 1 onion, coarse chopped
- 1 carrot, coarse chopped

Ingredient Group Two

- ½ cup sweet soy sauce
- 2 tbsp. sugar
- 2 tbsp. chopped scallions
- ½ tbsp. minced ginger

Ingredient Group Three

- 24 yellow square wonton wrappers
- ¼ cup Sriracha or chili paste
- 1 gallon of vegetable oil
- ½ cup sweet soy sauce

Directions

- Combine the wine, spices, garlic, sugar, and soy sauce from group one.

- Marinate the short ribs in this mixture for 3 hours.

- In a heavy-bottom pot on high heat, sear both sides of the short ribs in oil from group one and then add all of the marinade.

- Add water to three-quarters of the way up the short ribs.

- Add onion and carrot.

- Simmer and cook, covered, in a 450-degree oven for 2.5 hours until very tender, adding more water as needed.

- Remove from oven and let cool completely.

- Remove meat from pot and chop.

- Strain out cooking liquid.

- Combine meat with ingredients from group two.

- Place a tbsp. of meat filling into the middle of each wonton wrapper and moisten the edges with a little water. Fold up to seal and wrap the corners around the pouch like tortellini.

- Place them in refrigerator for 1 hour.

- Mix the Sriracha with the sweet soy from ingredient group three and set this aside as a dipping sauce.

- Heat up the vegetable oil in a pot to 325 degrees. Place the wontons in the hot oil from group three and cook till crisp, approximately 4 minutes. Remove, and blot any excess oil with a paper towel.

- Serve on a platter with the sauce.

I Cover the Waterfront: A Three-Course Seafood Buffet

Lobster Rolls

Frank Gotwals deftly eases the *Seasong*, his thirty-eight-foot lobstering boat, away from the dock in Stonington Harbor and heads for the open water of Maine's Penobscot bay. Dawn won't break for more than an hour and he's silhouetted by the glow of the boat's instruments, though after forty-five years of fishing these waters, he isn't relying on them to get where he's going. "It's like walking from my bedroom to my bathroom for me," Frank says. "I can do it blindfolded." As soon as he leaves the harbor, Gotwals hits the throttle, the powerful diesel engine erupts with a four-hundred-horsepower roar, and he squares his shoulders over his slightly staggered feet, leaning forward in a textbook fisherman's stance. Tall, wiry, his face unlined despite his decades on the water, Gotwals smiles frequently and laughs easily. At sixty-five, he says he's slowing down a bit, working only five days a week instead of six, taking winters off, but he still loves what is a very difficult job.

Long days. Brutally physical work. And a volatile market. "The most important rule of lobstering is to show up," he says. "One day will be up, one day will be down. One morning down, one afternoon up. You can't predict it. But one thing I know is true: you won't catch any lobster if you don't go."

The *Seasong* is about six miles from Stonington in fifty to sixty feet of water when the hard work begins. With a large metal grappling hook, Gotwals reaches over the side to grab one of his color-marked buoys, undoes the rope that connects it to a string of traps, attaches it to a powerful winch—so loud that he has to wear earplugs—and starts pulling them up. As each unwieldy, forty-or fifty-pound trap breaks the surface, he grabs it, hauls it aboard, then slides it down to his lone crewmember, sternwoman Alyssa LaPointe, to sort the keepers—if any—from everything else caught inside. It's a down day at first, a meager haul as Gotwals navigates from buoy to buoy, pulling up trap after trap. But as the day goes on, the catch improves. Nine lobsters in one trap alone, all keepers. LaPointe wraps their claws with rubber bands and drops them into a saltwater holding tank. All told, they'll bring in about 250 pounds of lobster, making it a break-even day. Gotwals will make enough to cover the cost of bait, fuel, and LaPointe's 20 percent share of the haul, but that leaves little room for profit. For him, anyway.

By the time today's catch makes its way to consumers, it will pass through many hands, each adding another cost to the eventual price. Every step of the supply chain—refrigerated trucking, cold storage, air freight, wholesaler markup, and restaurant costs and profit—results in a pound-and-a-quarter steamed lobster at many restaurants going for fifty or even sixty dollars. This has helped fuel the rise of the less expensive lobster roll. It's usually made from what's called processed lobster—claw, knuckle, and tail meat removed from the shell at an industrial facility, packed in plastic, and sold fresh or frozen, cooked or raw. For restaurants, using processed lobster eliminates the labor costs of kitchen employees steaming and shucking. And since those restaurants are often basic and unpretentious—as minimal as stands or even trucks—their total overhead is much lower than at white tablecloth establishments.

The lobster roll itself is a relatively simple dish—lobster meat in a hot dog bun. There are two basic styles. The Maine style is some combination of chilled lobster and mayonnaise in a New England style bun, which is split on top and crust-free on the sides to allow for grilling in butter. The Connecticut-style includes no mayo, and the lobster is served warm, drenched in butter, also on a New England style bun. Essential to both is just the right balance between the ingredients—the bun should not disappear under the weight and taste of the lobster, nor should it overwhelm them.

And in either form, it is a true classic. "Lobsters are really iconic American food," says culinary journalism legend Ruth Reichl, who's been both the *New York Times* restaurant critic and the editor of *Gourmet*. "Hamburgers, hot dogs, and pizza all came from somewhere else," she says. "The lobster roll didn't come from anywhere else. It is America on a bun." In the summer of 2009, Reichl put a gloriously photographed lobster roll on the cover of *Gourmet*. "We were a little late to the party. It would have been smarter if we had put it on a couple years earlier," she says. "What had happened in New York was Rebecca Charles opened Pearl in the late nineties and served this fantastic lobster roll that, at the time, it was the only lobster roll in New York City. By 2009, that restaurant had been copied so many times and it just seemed like, oh, this is a truly American dish and isn't it wonderful that it's having its moment?"

Yes, the lobster roll, born in New England, only became a "thing" after it was "discovered" in New York. Chef Rebecca Charles, who opened Pearl Oyster Bar in New York's Greenwich Village in 1997, is well aware of that fact. "Because I opened a restaurant in New York and not East Bumfuck it got noticed," she says. "If I had opened that restaurant somewhere else, it may never have happened that way." But it did. Soon, other restaurants were making lobster rolls of their own and Charles had ignited a national obsession. She says she was inspired by memories of family summers in Maine when she was growing up. She was never a big fan of the dish—she'd rather eat a whole steamed lobster instead—but she needed to put some sandwiches on the menu, never expecting the one filled with lobster to become such a massive hit.

And it is a remarkable creation. An overstuffed, grilled, top-loading hot dog bun; filled with a mixture of lobster, mayonnaise, finely diced celery, salt, and pepper; and topped with a squeeze of lemon. And unlike the vast majority of lobster rolls sold all across the country, this one does not begin with processed lobster meat. "They are made from the hundreds and hundreds of pounds of live lobster that we get deposited on our sidewalk every morning," Charles says. "The thing about a lobster roll is the lobster has to be really fresh. It has to be cooked properly, as in not overcooked. It's very easy to overcook lobster."

And easy to get too cute with it too, with cheffy twists and unusual ingredients. Charles says that's not her style. "It's not about spinning it so it's modern," she says. "It's just about elevating it, making it perfect, or as close to perfect as I can get it." Obsessing over every detail. "The bun has to be a certain color, golden brown," she says, "It can't be too dark, too light. It has to rest, covered, so that the inside of the bun steams, and it's very, very soft." As for the lobster, "It can't have too much mayonnaise or lemon juice. It can't be cut too big. It can't be cut too small. There's a certain range of size that I use that, I want people to see nice chunks, but I also want some of it be cut a little bit smaller, so that overall it has a certain texture. And it needs to be done the same way every time." That kind of time, care, and white tablecloth overhead isn't cheap. The lobster roll at Pearl costs thirty-four dollars, although in New York that isn't much more than many white tablecloth hamburgers. In much of the rest of the country, prices are often twenty dollars or more. And yet, the lobster roll can now be found almost everywhere.

In 2017, when Maine's *Down East* magazine ran a competition to select the best lobster roll in the world, the title was awarded to Freshie's Lobster Co. of Park City, Utah, owned by married, transplanted New Englanders Lorin and Ben Smaha. Their lobster roll is a kind of hybrid of the Maine and Connecticut styles. No mayo on the lobster. No butter on the bun. Just the opposite, in fact. "For me, lobster, putting butter on lobster is what it's all about," Lorin says. "Butter's on the lobster and we don't butter our bun." Instead, she uses a technique that's become popular for grilled cheese sandwiches. "We put mayo on the outside of the bun, and then grill the bun," she says. "I think it adds a little bit more flavor and kind of a little bit of that tanginess to the bun." And her take on the lobster roll has become so popular that Freshie's now has a second location in Salt Lake City and a third in Jackson Hole, Wyoming. She says, "After we won that award, it was all over the news for a while. And so, I think a lot of people came and tried it, which got them hooked and they got word of mouth, and all that stuff."

Their Salt Lake City location is in the Liberty Wells neighborhood, home to many young professionals and dotted with restaurants, coffee shops, and bars. The building is a converted single-family home, grey wood planks on the outside, airy and open to a high peaked ceiling inside, a lobster trap hanging over the door, and a pair of dark blue oars on the wall. And on this sunny September day, Angie Gallegos, fashionably dressed and sporting a colorful gold scarf, says she's here to defeat the calendar. "Summer is over, and I didn't want it to end," she says. "So, I thought a lobster roll would kind of extend it a little bit." And it seems to be working. "It really is so fresh," she says, "and I loved the textures. The texture between the crispy outside of the bun, the soft interior of the bun and the meat is so tender."

For his lobster roll, Morgan Broom, with tattoo sleeves on both arms and sunglasses pushed up on his head, ordered the spicy version with the lobster tossed in a Sriracha aioli and roasted red peppers and topped with chives. "It's got enough bite to it, and enough flavor and everything to it, that the spice isn't overpowering," he says. "It's so fresh and I didn't think that I would ever have lobster like that here in Utah." His fiancée Valerie Ventura says they come here, "as often as we want to treat ourselves."

That sense of indulgence is a big part of the lobster roll's appeal. It isn't cheap, but, for most people, it isn't out of reach. Says Jim Tselikis, cofounder of the Cousins Maine Lobster chain, "It's more expensive than a chicken sandwich, but it's less expensive than going to a five-star restaurant and having a one-and-a-quarter pound, one-and-a-half-pound steamed lobster that could cost you fifty dollars or sixty dollars." His cousin and company cofounder Sabin Lomac says simply, "They're an affordable luxury."

The cousins, who both grew up in Maine, began selling lobster rolls out of a single food truck in Los Angeles in 2012. Quickly invited to pitch potential investors on the television show *Shark Tank*, they convinced panelist Barbara Corcoran to invest $55,000. She suggested they franchise. Today, they have franchised thirty food trucks, as well as eleven restaurants, nationwide. Most are in places with no lobster roll history whatsoever, such as Birmingham, Columbus, Raleigh, Chattanooga, Phoenix, and Oklahoma City. Tselikis says, "Literally, there are places when we go to grand openings and to visit our franchisees, where customers are kind of wondering, what is a lobster roll?" Which is a unique challenge. "Part of the fun of our journey is being able to share that with them and kind of teach along the way."

And that makes Cousins food trucks mobile culinary classrooms. Large, jet-black, adorned with the Cousins logo—a big red lobster with the company name spelled out in white and red—the trucks contain full kitchens, including flattop grills and gas burners. The menu includes both a Maine-style lobster roll with mayo and a Connecticut-style roll with butter—their bestseller—as well as a variety of other lobster dishes, including lobster-topped tater tots, lobster mac-and-cheese, and a lobster quesadilla.

The lobster rolls are the priciest items, ranging anywhere from sixteen-fifty to nineteen dollars, depending on location. And that can be a challenge. Says Sabin, "A lot of people in LA or Phoenix or Dallas aren't used to lobster rolls, which is good from a perspective of they want to try it. However, there's a certain sense of shock when they see the price, even at seventeen dollars. If you go to Maine and you go to a reputable place, I would imagine you're not even going to find it for less than twenty."

Which means marketing the dish as something exceptional, like champagne. "There's something special about the accessibility of getting something that is incredibly unique and high class and celebratory," Sabin says. "When a girl calls you back or you got a raise or you're just having a great day and you feel like going to have something special that day, and with the case of the truck, the truck shows up outside of your building or it's in your neighborhood and you hear about it. It's something exciting to look forward to."

Cousins was not the first chain to bring lobster rolls from New England to the rest of the country. The pioneer, in fact, was co-owner Jim Tselikis's close childhood friend Luke Holden, who founded Luke's Lobster in 2009. Holden, living in New York and working in investment banking, was longing for the food he grew up with in Maine. "I was sitting at my desk on a summer Sunday afternoon missing home and I went online looking for something that reminded me of home," he says, "A traditional, Maine-style lobster roll. I couldn't find a roll that was in the right price range, of exceptional quality, and lobster-forward-tasting, nor served over anything but a white tablecloth type level of service."

So he created what was looking for, opening his first Luke's Lobster in Manhattan, adding more than thirty other locations since then—all company owned, no franchises. Their lobster rolls are Maine style—with mayo and a buttered, toasted bun. A roll containing four ounces of lobster—as big as or bigger than the rolls sold at most places—goes for seventeen dollars. A six-ounce roll costs twenty-two. And Luke's national impact has been enormous. As he puts it: "Over the last ten years, I think we have seen an explosion of lobster roll shacks because we have done exactly what Luke's set out to do, demystify and make lobster rolls more accessible to the general public." And inspire competitors. "You've had a handful of brains that have said, 'Hey, what those guys are doing is creating value for guests and they seem to be making money and having fun, so why don't we try it?' "

Holden's lobstering background stretches back to his childhood. "My dad had lobster pounds, lobster docks," he says. "I remember getting in trouble in school and, whenever that happened, Mom would drop me off at the docks to go work with Dad. That was my form of punishment. Little did she know, I loved doing that. So, it reinforced bad habits at school." Holden now owns his own lobster processing facility, providing his restaurants with pre-cooked lobster meat and selling a range of lobster products to retailers including Whole Foods. And he is developing a do-it-yourself lobster roll kit for them, which will include buns, lobster meat, butter, mayo, and seasoning. He already sells one online, as do a variety of companies. Luke's emphasizes their supply of lobsters is sustainable and caught by lobstermen they know. Cousins Lobster company says the same. And Holden predicts the lobster roll market will continue to grow. "There's just more and more demand," he says.

A growing customer base thrilled to have access to a wonderful, but once obscure regional dish. With a few exceptions. "I think it's really sad when you can get everything everywhere," Ruth Reichl says. "One of the great joys of eating is localness, and seasonalness. And so, being able to get a lobster roll in Utah is like eating strawberries in February."

But don't try telling that to the folks back at Freshie's, where pastry chef Amber Billingsley has come in for lunch. "This is my comfort food," she says. "The ability to just stop in, grab a lobster roll to go, then go sit underneath a tree just kind of blew my mind. It has become a sort of a ritual where I will treat myself maybe once a month to this decadent picnic that I do just for myself. Stopping in the midst of a stressful day and giving myself an hour to escape and sit in a quiet place to eat something so delicious is a luxurious form of self-care for me."

Oysters

It's a grey, gusty, and unseasonably chilly day in May along this stretch of the Delaware Bay in southern New Jersey. With low tide nearing, the beach in front of me is growing larger and larger. I'm being escorted through a hip-deep tidal pool to a series of sand bars that will disappear later in the day as the water rises. They are covered by dozens of what look like metal cot-frames. Sitting on top of each, securely attached by straps, is a mesh bag of oysters being cultivated here at the Cape May Salt Oyster Farm.

My guide, Cape May Salt's Melissa Harabedian, battling the whipping wind in a blue sweatshirt and wearing rubber boots, grabs one of the bags, slides off the piece of pipe keeping it closed, shakes out the oysters, and picks up a couple. "They are pretty oysters," she says. "One day they will be great market-sized oysters. They've got a nice round shape." In fact, for restaurants selling oysters on the half shell—which is the largest market—appearance matters. Misshapen shells don't look good on a tray of crushed ice. Nor does a big shell holding a tiny oyster. The oyster farmers here apply specific techniques to get what they need—healthy, meaty oysters that are visually pleasing—by ensuring they can grow unimpeded and get all of the microscopic nutrients they need from the water. It begins with tending to the oysters every day, hosing them down to keep them from smothering in muck, and periodically bringing them back to home base for further maintenance.

"We actually run them through what's called a tumbler," says General Manager Brian Harman. "It turns the oysters in a drum, and it washes them and cleans them." Leaving the tumbler, the oysters are sorted by size. They can then be moved to new bags to reduce crowding and give them plenty of room to grow. And the larger the oysters, the larger the mesh in the bags. "The bigger the mesh, the more water flow, the more food availability and the better they grow," says Harman. Tumbling also knocks the oysters into each other, knocking off the ragged edges of new shell growth. "You're like pruning the oyster," Harman says, "and that really encourages it to grow thicker, fatter and a deeper cup, so that when you shuck it and you have that meat in there, there's more room for the meat, it can fill out. And it fills the shell completely."

Oysters, like wine, taste the way they do because of where they are grown. The salinity of the water, the algae in it, the minerals, the temperature, and more. These oysters are also impacted by being grown in tidal pools, exposed to the elements for several hours a day, and buffeted by the tides. Cape May Salt also grows oysters a couple of miles out in the bay, in cages twenty feet down, tended by boat. And that environment gives them a significantly different flavor.

When they first began farming here in 1997, Cape May Salt harvested two hundred thousand oysters a year. The haul has since grown to three million. According to the most recent national statistics from 2017, oyster farms sold more than three-hundred-million pounds of oysters that year, bringing producers $186 million in revenue. And 95 percent of all the oysters consumed in America are farmed, bringing back what once seemed like an inexhaustible resource, until it was close to being wiped out.

There is archeological evidence of oysters in what became America as far back as ten-thousand years ago. When the first explorers and settlers from England arrived, they were astonished by just how immensely plentiful they were. Both the Chesapeake Bay and the waters around New York City were teeming with oysters, billions of them, miles of oyster reefs as much as twenty feet high. And the oysters themselves were massive, some reaching a foot or more in length. Native Americans had long eaten them. Now the newcomers would do the same, and they became a mainstay of the American diet. In a letter to a friend in 1786, George Washington told him, "Mrs. Washington joins me in thanking you for your kind present of pickled oysters which were very fine."

By the mid to late nineteenth century, the country was oyster obsessed, nowhere more so than New York, where the local waters produced seven hundred million oysters in a year. They were sold on the streets, in extravagant restaurants, as well as at oyster houses, where a bottomless order of all-you-can eat raw oysters cost six cents. Total. Not per oyster. The newly completed transcontinental railroad made them available throughout the country. Oyster bars opened in the most landlocked of cities. The oyster trade on the Gulf coast, which had lagged behind both the East and West Coasts, had ramped up. It was an oyster boom.

But in the twentieth century, overfishing, disease, and especially pollution would put an end to it. Production and consumption would decline precipitously over the years. Oysters fell out of favor for decades until a combination of factors brought the industry back. Polluted waters being cleaned up. The development of oyster farms. And a growing number of chefs championing a fresher, healthier diet.

By the 1980s, the oyster bar began a quiet resurgence which became a boom of its own. And in recent years, Americans have once again fallen deeply in love with the oyster. At oyster bars and seafood restaurants, but also at many restaurants that don't feature much seafood at all, a plate of a dozen fresh oysters on the half shell is a menu staple. Buck-a-shuck oysters, a dollar apiece, are a feature at happy hours across the country.

"It's just become like a trendy thing," Harman says. "It seems like it's always been sort of an older person's thing and as it's caught on to like younger crowds, it's just exploded and they're everywhere." And from everywhere. "You can go to an oyster bar and try ten different varieties from all over the country or all over the world," he says, "and you're sort of like visiting that bay, you know? It's kind of like going on a little trip, sort of."

College student Morgan Pruitt is taking that trip over lunch at the Plank Seafood Provisions restaurant in Omaha, Nebraska. "I'm glad that I got to try so many different types today," she says. "It was two varieties from Massachusetts, one from Virginia, and one from Canada. And one was a river oyster, which I'd never had before, and I think the best way to describe it was, it was really fresh. It was just like a capsule of water in my mouth."

Plank is known for its variety of fresh oysters, offering several types from different places every day, all arrayed on piles of crushed ice in a glass case along one end of a large, three-sided, granite-topped oyster bar. Behind the bar, holding an oyster down with his mesh-glove clad left hand, popping the hinge that keeps the shell closed with a stubby knife in his right hand, Thomas Kerns assembles the "Walk the Plank," a dozen-oyster sampler of different varieties. Before he came here two years ago, the laid-back thirty-two-year-old, who grew up in a tiny town at the southwest corner of Nebraska, had never even tasted an oyster. Now, he says, "I can do this with my eyes closed."

Plank serves between five hundred and seven hundred fresh oysters every day. They're shipped in several times a week from a variety of suppliers. And it is the sophistication of the supply chain that has developed over recent years—fast, efficient shipping from the water to the restaurant—that has made the oyster boom possible. Here in Omaha, what first attracted transplants from out of town now entices born and bred locals as well. Co-owner Tony Gentile, who grew up eating oysters on the Gulf Coast, says, "It's just been an education process with several factors involved. One of them being somebody in a social group saying, 'Oh my gosh, you've never had oysters? You have to try them.' "

Five species of oysters are grown in North America. From them come more than 150 varieties, differentiated by location, which determines their taste. These are some of the most common varieties to be found on oyster bar and restaurant menus.

Beausoleil

Light, delicate, mildly briny flavor. Yeasty, champagne-like
aroma. Uniform shells, two-and-a-half inches across. From New
Brunswick, Canada.

Blue Point

Mild-flavored with medium salinity and minerality. Three to four
inches across, relatively round shell.

True Blue Points are harvested in Long Island Sound, though
the name is often applied to other Atlantic oysters.

Kumamoto

Sweet, fruity, somewhat nutty flavors. Around two inches across,
with a fluted, deep-cupped shell. From Washington and California.

Malpeque

Salty, briny, with iron and mineral taste. Teardrop-shaped, two to
four inches across. From Prince Edward Island, Canada.

Olympia

Creamy textured with coppery, metallic flavor and medium
salinity. As small as a quarter, usually less than two inches
across. From Washington state.

Wellfleet

Briny, yet also sweet. Heavy shells. Up to three-and-a-half inches
across. From Wellfleet Harbor in northeastern Cape Cod.

Oysters don't have to be raw. Americans have been enjoying cooked
oysters since colonial times—in chowder, in sauce, pan roasted,
broiled, fricasseed, escalloped, fried, as patties, croquettes, in
oyster pie, in turkey dressing, pickled, and more. The historic Acme

Oyster house in New Orleans serves millions of raw oysters every year but those aren't their bestseller. Monique Ricci, whose family owns the 110-year-old restaurant, says their most popular oysters are char-grilled. "The easiest way that most people who have never, ever eaten an oyster will always try them char-grilled," she says. "It kind of takes away the scariness of eating a raw oyster. You just drench them in butter and garlic and cheese, and anything will be good with that." And there is still enough of a local oyster population that these are not farmed, they are harvested from natural oyster beds by local fishermen. "People just want to come and get a Louisiana oyster. There's this something different to ours," Ricci says, "They're better. They're way better."

And great on another New Orleans favorite, a po' boy. It's a sandwich made on special French bread, usually from the Leidenheimer Baking Company, that is both crusty on the outside and soft on the inside. Once a Gulf specialty, po' boys are now available throughout the rest of the country. Kansas. Oklahoma. Arizona. Indiana. Virtually everywhere. Leidenheimer even ships their fresh bread to thirty-two states and Washington, DC. But to Ricci, po' boys should be eaten where they were born. "You're never going to get the same product that we get, and we've just been doing it for too long," she says. "I mean that's like going down to Florida and getting a lobster roll. You've got to go to Maine to get that stuff. It's just not the same." Though, as we've already seen, lobster rolls are now everywhere. And so are po' boys.

And some of the restaurateurs serving them got help from a New Orleans po' boy legend, Marvin Matherne. He has been making some of New Orleans' best po' boys for twenty-seven years at Guy's, a small, bright blue, wood-slatted building at the corner of Magazine and Valmont streets. He says he gets calls all the time from restaurateurs—or would-be restaurateurs—asking how to make them properly. "I tell them how. I never, ever don't share my knowledge with somebody," he says, "because it's a wonderful sandwich. Why shouldn't people be able to have it every day, every week, whatever they want? You shouldn't have to travel just to New Orleans to get a sandwich."

And done right, the oyster po' boy is truly a thing—a taste—of beauty. "Think about a raw oyster on a half shell. Without doing anything, it's unbelievable," Matherne says. "Now, taking it and dipping it in some corn flour and frying it. That can't really hurt it, right?"

Caviar

Salted fish eggs called roe, removed from sturgeon and eaten raw. To some, it sounds disgusting. To others, it represents the height of luxury. As with oysters, the American caviar supply once seemed boundless. In the nineteenth century, so much caviar was being harvested from sturgeon taken from the Delaware river, and eventually the Great Lakes as well, that bars gave it away for free—the saltiness would cause customers to order more drinks. Late in the century, America produced more caviar than any other country on earth. Most went to Europe. Much of it came back, fraudulently sold as caviar from Russia, which commanded a much higher price. And so much was consumed that by the 1920s, the American caviar supply had been all fished out.

For the next eight decades, the world's caviar came almost entirely from the Caspian Sea—from the Soviet Union and, to a lesser degree, Iran. Conditions in the Caspian were perfect for sturgeon, a bizarre looking fish covered in bony plates instead of scales and almost unchanged since prehistoric times. There are more than two dozen varieties of sturgeon throughout the world. The Caspian varieties prized for caviar are the Osetra, the Sevruga, and the largest and most prized of all, the Beluga, a massive fish which can reach more than fifteen feet in length and weigh more than a ton. Its caviar consists of large, soft, shiny eggs ranging from grey to deep black in color.

After the Soviet Union collapsed in 1991, strict government controls over the caviar industry fell apart. By 2006, Caspian sturgeon were so dangerously overfished, the stock so gutted, that a worldwide ban was instituted. With the world's best now unavailable, the only answer was farmed caviar from sturgeon raised in captivity. Caviar connoisseurs had long dismissed that as inferior. But now, there was nothing else. Realistically, the initial caviar harvested from American species such as paddlefish and hackleback could not compete with caviar from the Caspian, but Sevruga and Osetra farmed here from Russian bloodlines turned out to be excellent. Still, the caviar long considered the best of all, Beluga, remained completely unavailable in America. Until 2020. It's a saga that began almost two decades earlier.

In 1983, Ukrainian immigrant Mark Zaslavsky opened a gourmet food store in Miami. By the early 2000s, he had built a successful business selling high-end specialty foods, including caviar from Russia. With Caspian sturgeon stocks disappearing, but before the ban was put in place, he imported around fifty live sturgeon to Florida from the Caspian Sea, intent on producing caviar at a 120-acre caviar farm he named Sturgeon Aquafarms. "He kind of foresaw all of this," says his grandson David Bashkov, who runs the farm. "It was three, four trips that he took over to the countries surrounding the Caspian Sea. [He] put the fish on a flight on Lufthansa and brought them over here." About half of them were the elite Beluga variety. Incredibly, while others imported various Caspian sturgeon, no one else brought in any of the treasured Beluga. When the ban took effect, Zaslavsky had the only Beluga sturgeon anywhere in the United States.

They would not be used for caviar, however, since the fish is killed during the harvesting process. Instead, they would become brood stock. It would take years for them to reach maturity and breed. Some of their offspring would be used to help rebuild the world's sturgeon population. The rest would be used, after they began producing eggs of their own, for the production of caviar. "It's a huge investment and it's a lot of patience," Bashkov says. "The whole process took about seventeen years." Finally, in 2020, after an additional delay when Hurricane Michael destroyed some of their stock, the waiting was over, and the first harvest began, starting with a beautiful fish, fifty-six kilos in weight and more than six feet long.

"I actually extracted the eggs from the fish myself," Bashkov says. "I did the whole process of salting, curing the eggs. So, I actually saw, tasted, and experienced the whole spectrum from the very, very beginning." Bashkov is in his twenties. He was in grade school when the importation ban took effect, so he had never tasted Beluga caviar before. It was a revelation. "I've tried so many different caviars from different farms," he says, "I've never tried something like Beluga. It's extremely creamy and delicate with a very rich flavor profile. The best part of the Beluga caviar is its pure beginning and finishing notes. It's just different from any other caviar."

So is the price. $830 an ounce—doing the math, that's more than
$11,000 a pound—though for those on a budget, it is available
by the half-ounce as well. And there is a market for it. Bashkov
says, "We had customers for so many years asking, 'When is the
Beluga going to be ready? When is it going to be ready?' So, we are
selling the caviar. There is, I would say, a very, very high interest in
the caviar."

The caviar is sold under the Marky's brand, along with several
other less expensive caviars, from Sevruga and Osetra to American
White sturgeon; hackleback, which is also a form of sturgeon native
to America; paddlefish, similar to sturgeon but a different species;
bowfin, a fish whose roe has a history in Cajun cuisine; and more.
It's the kind of assortment now offered by numerous other caviar
farms in what has become a growing industry. Not just in America,
but all over the world. In fact, the single largest supplier of caviar is
now China.

At the opulent London Chop House in Detroit, they serve Osetra
caviar farmed in Italy. One ounce with various garnishes and a
shot of Stolichnaya vodka, brought to one's leather banquette in
the gilded dining room, costs $150. Executive Chef Robert Scherer
says, "I think there's two reasons" people order it.

"And I'm going to use my father as one. He is not a foodie. And
I don't even think he even knows what fish produces caviar. But
when he sees it on a menu, about 50 percent of the time he'll order
it. He orders it because he thinks it's fancy. He thinks it's cool.
And it's a highlight for him because of the price point and it's like a
treat. So, I think there's people like that, that enjoy just the treat of
it. And then there's another group of people that really appreciate
the caviar for what it is, and the fact that it takes ten years for the

fish to develop till harvest and how big of a delicacy that it really can be. And those people appreciate it for more of the tradition and the skill and the patience that goes into actually producing it." Scherer says in an admittedly culinarily conservative city, he sells between six and ten caviar services a month. He fantasizes about the price dropping at some point, making the delicacy available to more people, but isn't holding his breath.

The most accessible market for caviar is online. Hackleback can be found for twenty-four dollars an ounce. So can paddlefish. Osetra from the well-respected Marshallberg Farm ranges from $48 to $240 an ounce. The founder of that farm, IJ Won says, "People do seem to like us because they are willing to pay what we ask for." His sales have reached a million dollars a year, though Won, trained as a scientist, says he started the farm not to make money, but as an exercise in sustainability, and certainly not out of any love for caviar. He explains, "Do I like it? I wouldn't pay for it."

The Pearl Oyster Bar Lobster Roll

Chef/owner Rebecca Charles made the lobster roll a national sensation with this recipe.

Ingredients

- 4 1¼ lb. lobsters, cooked and shelled, preferably culls[1]
- ½ rib of celery, finely minced
- ½–¾ cup Hellmann's mayonnaise (Rebecca's preference)
- squeeze of lemon juice
- salt and pepper to taste
- 4 top-loading hot dog buns (preferably Pepperidge Farm)
- 4 tbsp. unsalted butter
- chopped chives

Directions

- Place lobsters in a large pot of rapidly boiling water. 1 to 1¼ pound lobsters will take from 7 to 10 minutes, 1 to 1½ pound lobsters, 10 to 12 minutes, and will float when done. Immerse them in an ice bath for 10 minutes to stop the cooking and cool thoroughly. Remove and drain.

- Separate the tail and claw from the body. Lightly crush the tail with the heel of your hand to crack the shell. Bend the sides of the shell back and remove the tail in one piece. Separate the claw from the knuckle. Hold the claw in one hand and whack the top with the back of a chef's knife, giving the blade a little twist at the end to separate the shell into two pieces. Wiggle the thumb meat back and forth and pull it off. Pull the claw meat out. With the small end of a fork or spoon, pry the meat out of the upper portion of the knuckle. Put the spoon end in again and break off that piece of empty shell. Now, pry the meat out of the remaining piece of shell. Cut the tail in half lengthwise, pull out the digestive tract, then pull the claw meat apart and remove cartilage.

---

1 If you have access to them, culls are lobsters that have lost or damaged a claw and are less expensive. Make sure that whatever size you buy, the lobsters are feisty and lively.

→

- Chop into ½" to ¾" pieces. Put meat in a bowl with the rest of the ingredients and mix until combined. Don't over mix. Cover and chill. For best results, don't make more than one day in advance.

- Melt 4 Tbsp. unsalted butter over low-medium heat in a ten-inch sauté pan. Place hot dog buns on their sides in the butter and toast until golden brown. Flip buns over a couple of times so that both sides soak up an equal amount of butter and brown evenly. Add a bit more butter if necessary.

- Fill the bun with the lobster salad and sprinkle it with chopped chives. At Pearl, we serve it with a big stack of shoestring fries and a garnish of baby greens. In Maine, the traditional garnish is a couple of slices of bread-and-butter pickles and a bag of potato chips.

Ice Cream—America's Favorite Treat

A warm wind whips through the open cab as Garrett "Sully" Sullivan guides his white 1959 Good Humor ice cream truck down a Connecticut road by the Long Island Sound. From the fifties through the seventies, trucks just like this one—essentially a boxy, white freezer on wheels, with no roof or doors on the driver's compartment—were a familiar sight all over the country, roaming through neighborhoods, attracting hordes of kids, who'd enjoy their Good Humor bars together while hanging out, often sitting on the curb. Sully was one of them.

"I remember this truck actually from when I was younger playing little league," he says. The man who owned it back then was known to everyone as Papa Joe. "I remember him going around town and ringing the bell and selling ice cream and having a smile on his face." After Papa Joe retired, Sully got an opportunity to buy the truck, surprising his wife, and perhaps himself, with an impulse purchase steeped in memories. And not just his memories. "I used to go with Papa Joe," exclaims a mom buying ice cream for her son at Sully's first stop of the day. "This was my truck! We used to see him and his dog and we loved it. Yeah, he was the best."

As Sully drives his route, people wave and smile. "That's the best part of it," he says. "I love it! Everyone loves it." At one stop, two young sisters run up, screaming, to get their SpongeBob popsicles. Their grandmother reminisces, "That bell was just as exciting to us as it is to kids today." The father of a young toddler remembers the ice cream truck in his neighborhood when he was growing up. "If I heard it, I would run outside," he says, "It was something I could afford with my own money, supposedly." A mom says simply, "Ice cream makes everyone happy." And it has for hundreds of years.

"It's so interwoven and blended in with our history," says Amy Ettinger, who wrote *Sweet Spot: An Ice Cream Binge Across America.* "George Washington was a huge ice cream lover and I think for the founding fathers, for them it was about the innovation of it. It was like, this is this new thing that Thomas Jefferson brought over from France. And so, it has that as well. It's not just the comfort but it's the sense of we're Americans and we're innovators and we're on the cutting edge of things."

While flavored frozen concoctions can be traced back to China's Tang Dynasty (AD 618–907), the earliest known recipe for something close to the ice cream of today, which is generally a frozen combination of butterfat and solids from milk and cream, sweeteners, and flavorings, with air whipped in, dates from the late 1690s in Italy. The new delicacy spread among the aristocracy in Europe and Britain, and then the United States. Jeri Quinzio, who wrote *Of Sugar and Snow: A History of Ice Cream Making,* says, "It was very expensive and only pretty much wealthy people were able to afford ice cream." Sugar was costly. Access to ice was limited to those who could afford to build an icehouse to store a supply harvested from a local river. And even for those who could afford it, the process of making ice cream required substantial physical labor.

Over time, however, technology was developed, such as the hand-cranked ice cream freezer, patented in 1843, mechanical refrigeration and freezing, and improved transcontinental transportation, that would change everything. "Americans made ice cream an everyday treat for an ordinary person." Quinzio says, "It became commercial and readily available and pretty much everyone could have it." And they embraced it as quintessentially American. Ettinger says, "It was one of the first things that immigrants into Ellis Island were given." As they began their new lives in overcrowded tenements in squalid neighborhoods, they would find vendors called hokey pokey men—despite various theories, the origin of the name is unclear—peddling ice cream on the streets from glass dishes shared, with little or no thought given to sanitation, by customer after customer.

Ice cream quickly became a common denominator between rich and poor. The *New York Sun* reported in 1900 that Wall Street brokers were enjoying the newly created ice cream sandwich "in a democratic fashion side by side on the sidewalk with the messengers and the office boys. Blue and white collars alike huddled around pushcarts on hot summer days."

There would be milestone after milestone. The ice cream cone became a sensation at the World's Fair of 1904 and kicked off a boom in ice cream consumption nationwide. The Eskimo Pie, a block of vanilla ice cream covered in chocolate, was created in 1921 and was soon one-upped by the Good Humor bar, a similar product on a stick, which was far less messy to eat. Good Humor was sold from a fleet of white freezer-equipped trucks. During prohibition, ice cream parlors replaced many bars and brewers made ice cream instead of beer. By 1930, ice cream was everywhere.

It was considered so important for America's troops to get ice cream during World War Two that an ice cream manufacturing plant was set up on a barge in the South Pacific. Military doctors prescribed ice cream to help soldiers recover from combat fatigue. Back at home, ice cream manufacturers coped with rationing of ingredients by stretching what they had. And then, Quinzio says, "Ice cream makers realized that afterward that they could get away with more air, less cream, or less rich ice cream because people got used to it."

By the fifties, with consumers shopping mainly by price, ice cream manufacturers were producing a low-cost product that just qualified as ice cream under federal law. Butterfat levels as low as 10 percent, the lowest allowable. Overrun, the amount of air in the ice cream as high as 100 percent—the most allowable—which meant half of the product was air. By comparison, today's best ice creams can contain as much as 18 or 19 percent butterfat and as little as 20 percent air. Also helping to keep prices low in the fifties, the quality of ingredients in ice cream was reduced. And as more and more ice cream was being sold at supermarkets, where shelf life was key, emulsifiers and stabilizers were added. For a long time, that was the formula for almost all of the ice cream sold in America.

But in recent years, America has been enjoying an ice cream revolution, a kind of golden age. From perfectly serviceable economy gallons to high-butterfat, low overrun, so-called premium and super-premium ice creams; unusual flavors and add-ins; low fat, high protein, added-benefit, and vegan varieties; and artisanal ice cream, often with handmade ingredients and requiring the culinary skills of a classically trained chef.

"There's an expectation there from the consumer that they'll have a wide variety of choices," says Matt Herrick of the International Dairy Foods Association. "They'll have fifteen or twenty different options when it just comes to a potato chip. They'll have fifteen or twenty different options when it comes to coffee, and the same is true for dairy products. I mean, especially for ice cream, when they walk into the ice cream case, they want not only different flavors and different specialty additives like candy, or chocolate chunks, or things like that, but they also want lower fat varieties. They may want frozen yogurt. They may want a plant-based ice cream. They may want it in pint sizes versus gallon or half gallons."

The average American eats more than twenty pounds of ice cream a year. That adds up to 1,000,400,000 gallons, an eleven-billion-dollar a year business. The bestselling brand is Ben & Jerry's, with an annual revenue of more than $680 million. Now owned by massive conglomerate Unilever, it began as a single shop opened on May 5, 1978, in a converted gas station in Burlington, Vermont, by Ben Cohen and Jerry Greenfield. Not that they felt a burning desire to make ice cream. That would come later.

"Ben and I grew up together," Greenfield says, "Ben dropped out of several colleges, I tried to get into medical school, never got in. So, we thought we would just do something together. We'd always liked to eat, we wanted to pick a food that was becoming popular in cities but had not yet been brought to college towns. And at that time, we identified bagels and homemade ice cream. And we checked out bagel making equipment. It was more money than we had, so we figured ice cream had to be cheaper, and so we picked ice cream."

Their timing was perfect. "The quality of ice cream had been deteriorating," Greenfield says, "and to a certain degree, mainstream ice cream still is deteriorating." Complete novices, they signed up for a correspondence course on ice cream making from Penn State University, read a textbook on the subject, visited a variety of scoop shops for field research, and went to work.

"It was extremely chaotic," Greenfield says, "We had no idea what we were doing. Every day was a complete adventure." But they were clear on what they wanted to make. "We wanted it to be very creamy, we wanted it to be all natural, we wanted it to be great flavors," Greenfield says, "So, it was not saying, 'Oh, we're going to put in 15 percent butterfat, and blah, blah, blah,' it was much more by taste, quality, and the naturalness of the ingredients." And the power of the flavors, for a highly unusual reason—Ben Cohen had a limited sense of smell and taste, so they flavored the ice creams heavily as a result.

And Greenfield credits a couple of inspirations: Reuben Mattus, who created Häagen-Dazs which, in the early seventies, became the first widely available brand of ice cream marketed as premium; and Steve Herrell, who began making his own ice cream in 1973 at Steve's Ice Cream in Somerville, Massachusetts. It was Herrell who is generally credited with popularizing mix-ins, bits of candy, cookies, or other treats added to ice cream (though chocolate chip had been around for decades and Rocky Road was created after the stock market crash of 1929 to represent the path to better times).

"A candy that I'd come to really love was Heath Bars," Herrell says, "and I thought, these would be great in ice cream. But what flavor?" He decided to leave that to each customer. "We'll put a scoop of the ice cream flavor of their choice down on the board, and see what they want mixed in," he says. "And we can have other things mixed in too. M&Ms, broken up cookies, broken brownies, whatever, as well as fruit and nuts. And so, on opening day at Steve's Ice Cream in Somerville, halfway between Harvard and Tufts, on opening day in 1973, we did ice cream mix-ins. And people just went bananas over it and loved it."

Herrell added the extras while each customer was waiting. Ben & Jerry's took the idea even further and began mixing them in when the ice cream was first made. Greenfield insists that, to this day, no one else does it as well: "Ben & Jerry's has been making ice cream like this since the company started in 1978. And since it first packaged ice cream in the early eighties. So, it's been almost forty years. And yet, there's no other ice cream company that has figured out how to package ice cream with big chunks of cookies and candies in the way that Ben & Jerry's does." In more than two dozen varieties at any one time, such as Everything But The...—vanilla and chocolate ice creams with peanut butter cups, white chocolate chunks, fudge-covered almonds, and fudge-covered toffee pieces; Sweet Like Sugar Cookie Dough Core—almond flavored sweet cream ice cream, cherry ice cream with cherries, shortbread cookies, and a sugar cookie dough core; Punch Line—cherries and roasted almonds in almond and brown butter bourbon ice creams; Cinnamon Buns—cinnamon bun dough and a cinnamon streusel swirl in caramel ice cream; and perhaps their most famous flavor, Cherry Garcia—cherry ice cream with cherries and fudge flakes.

Today, mix-ins are an ice cream staple at the highest and lowest ends of the price and quality spectrums—which do not always correlate. In fact, over time, the flavor palate of American ice cream has expanded exponentially, especially among so-called premium or even super-premium brands, marketed as higher quality and as being more carefully produced, and with significantly more butterfat and less air.

"I think it became chic and trendy, is one thing," Jeri Quinzio says, "I'm not sure how much of it was the result of someone sitting down and saying, 'Let me taste this next to the ice cream I bought at the supermarket for half the price and this is better,' or in how much of it was just, 'Oh, I heard that there's this exciting new ice cream on the market. Let's try it.' "

Food industry analyst David Portalatin says, "American consumers today are really into what I call permissive indulgence." In other words, finding a way to banish the guilt: "I'm having ice cream, but at least I'm putting something of quality into my body. It's made with very authentic ingredients in a very traditional or artisanal fashion. Or something of that nature. So, it's really all about feeling better about what you're eating," says Portalatin.

Donna Berry, who writes an online dairy industry newsletter, says, "When we're going to indulge, we want something good." And she says, "We're willing to pay more for less that's better quality." Up to ten dollars a pint, in some cases. An affordable luxury.

Quinzio says, "It's not that much more. It's not like buying diamonds or something." And plenty of customers are willing to pay the price for top-shelf brands such as Jeni's, Van Leeuwen, Tillamook, and more. Jerry Greenfeld says, "I think there's a limit as to how much money people will pay for ice cream. But I could be wrong. I'll tell you that I remember many, many, many years ago when Ben & Jerry's first went over two dollars a pint in supermarkets, and we were shaking in our boots that people were going to stop buying ice cream when a pint went over two dollars. And sure enough, people continued to eat ice cream."

Many of the high-end brands now made commercially in volume began in small scoop shops. And it is in today's so-called artisanal ice cream shops that the most creative ice cream makers are extending boundaries, often by combining ice cream with haute cuisine. "We've always treated it more as a fine dining experience," says Tyler Malek, the head ice cream maker at Salt & Straw ice cream, which he opened with his cousin in Portland, Oregon, in 2011, and which now has stores in six cities. Malek, young, slight of build, and partial to T-shirts and baseball caps, is renowned for making some of the finest and most creative ice cream anywhere in the country.

"We make all of our ice cream by hand," he says. And almost everything that goes into it. "I'd say like 95 percent of everything we put in the ice cream is made from scratch in our kitchen. We kind of realized that pretty early on in our career, in my career at least, that that was super important because we have to alter every recipe so that it freezes and it integrates into the ice cream just perfectly. On top of this idea, there's no one out there making, you know, candied olive brittle out in the world. So, we have to write our own recipes from that perspective." Using artisanal and local ingredients. In batches as small as five gallons. Such as Pear and Blue Cheese ice cream made with candied Oregon Bartlett pears and blue cheese from Oregon's Rogue Creamery. Black Olive Brittle and Goat Cheese ice cream made with organic California coast olives and cave-aged Humboldt Fog goat cheese. He even demonstrates how to make a variety of his flavors, step by step, in a series of online videos. Viewers can watch Malek carefully tempering egg yolks in hot cream for a buttermilk custard ice cream base, coating crispy bacon with homemade caramel candy, tearing apart fluffy blueberry pancakes, and combining it all with maple syrup to create Buttermilk Pancakes, Bacon, and Eggs ice cream. Dropping a fresh habanero pepper into a saucepan of deep purple Oregon marionberries as they cook into a jam for Goat

Cheese Marionberry Habanero ice cream. Mixing sour cream into cream cheese, coating hazelnuts with caramelized butter and sugar, and roasting candied carrots for Carrot Cake Batter with Praline Hazelnut ice cream.

"I'm so intent on this idea of telling different stories with the ice cream." Malek says. Collaborating with famed San Francisco chef Traci Des Jardins, known for epic culinary creations, Malek's challenge was "to basically use her same voice and the style and techniques to get the different textures and swirls and beauty in the ice cream." Which resulted in a flavor called Duck Crackling with Cherry Preserves, made of duck fat ice cream with molasses and salted custard, candied duck skin brittle, honey gastrique, and scratch-made tart cherry preserves.

Then again, perfection need not be complicated. "On the flip side," Malek says, "if we're working with an amazing farmer that's growing these strawberries that you can only get for like three days out of the year, and the strawberries have this intense fruitiness, a little spicy, you don't want to, we don't put anything in that." Really. Here's Malek's entire recipe: "It's just a little bit of cream, a little bit of sugar, and blend it into strawberries and put it in the ice cream machine."

It's a pleasant, brisk mid-November evening on Hayes Street in San Francisco. The smell of fresh waffle cones drifts out of the open-doored, glass front of the Salt & Straw ice cream shop there. Inside, the counter crew, including one young woman with orange hair and glittery green eye makeup, are filling orders in front of four wood-framed chalkboards listing the flavors.

Repeat customer David Wang has his usual, a scoop of Chocolate Brownie and one of Honey Lavender. "This is my forty-fourth time getting these same two," he says. And what keeps him coming back again and again? "I think it's really the Honey Lavender. It's hard to find anywhere else," he says. "I haven't really had such a fragrant kind of ice cream before."

Vince Nguyen has gone for the Caramel Ribbons with Cookie Dough. "I really love the salty caramel," he says, "I think salt is hard to do without it tasting like you just licked a grain of salt and they do it really well. It's dispersed and deliciously permeates the whole thing."

Maxwell Morris, here with his friend Hunter Dean, says, "We're just like obsessed with this ice cream, I got Candycopia." Morris explains that it's "a butterscotch ice cream with just, like, literally every candy bar you can throw in it." Except the candy, mimicking Heath Bars, Reese's Peanut Butter Cups, Snickers, and Whoppers, is made from scratch.

Malek says, "When we're brainstorming a flavor in our kitchen, in our R&D room, literally the only limit is how many hands can we fit around the ice cream machine. For example, if we have one hand that's like sprinkling in this certain type of cookie and this other hand that's piping in this marshmallow fluff, and another hand that's ribboning in a homemade jam, how many people can you fit around the machine? We've gotten up to thirteen hands for a test flavor. We've actually, manufacturing, we've done the nine-hand flavor." It was called the Universe, an ode to the big bang theory—the real one, not the sitcom—a dark black ice cream with various add-ins representing the planets and the rest of the universe.

And since it is mid-November, they're featuring Thanksgiving flavors with ingredients including crisped turkey skin, sweet potato, and cranberries. Even a take on stuffing. "I got the Roasted Peach and Cornbread Stuffing," says Cloie Von Massenhausen, who used to live in San Francisco and is back visiting. "I love peaches, so it brings out a lot of the sweetness of them rather than tart, especially since it's not peach season right now, which is really nice. And then it has little chunks of cornbread [cookies], almost like corn meal, so it gives it some texture that's really nice. And then the ice cream itself is just insanely creamy." Brandt Hill got a scoop of that one, and a scoop of Sea Salt and Caramel. He says, "I like to go adventurous for one, and then stick with the classics for the other."

Of late, Tyler Malek's adventurousness has taken him into a whole new arena—making vegan ice cream with no milk products. Purists will say it isn't ice cream at all since it has no butterfat, but Malek is excited about breaching yet another frontier: "Making the most indulgent, thoughtful, and creative vegan ice cream in the world. Like Peanut Butter Captain Munch. Sarah Beck, who lives just a couple of blocks away, loves it: "It was like the old-school Captain Crunch cereal and it was just the best thing I've ever had."

Maxwell Morris says, "I even order vegan items like today without even knowing they're vegan." That would be the mint chocolate chip on top of his scoop of Candycopia. He didn't realize it was dairy-free until he was told, after he tasted it. "That's how good it is," he says.

In fact, vegan or dairy-free ice cream—more accurately called frozen dessert to conform with federal regulations—is hot these days. Nationwide, companies such as Coconut Bliss, So Delicious, Ripple, and NadaMoo are targeting the vegan and dairy-free markets—not always the same thing, given the difference between lactose intolerance and an ethical aversion to animal products—replacing butterfat with fats from a variety of nondairy sources, such as coconuts, almonds, cashews, oats, and soy. Cado brand even uses avocado.

And beyond the niche producers, many well-known ice cream companies have entered the dairy-free market with flavors of their own, including Jeni's, Breyer's, Baskin-Robbins, and Häagen-Dazs. Ben & Jerry's cofounder Jerry Greenfield says dairy-free is fine by him. "I don't want to sound flippant about this, but no, I don't really care," he says, "I'm not an ice cream purist. I would say I'd like any of those products to be high quality." Ben & Jerry's itself has more than a dozen flavors of nondairy ice cream now, made with almond milk or sunflower butter instead of butterfat, including a nondairy Cherry Garcia, Crème Brûlée Cookie, and Caramel Almond Brittle. Having sold the company, Greenfield and Ben Cohen no longer make product decisions, but he says he's happy to see the new pints. "I was very excited and still am very excited about it," he says.

In fact, going vegan is just one of many efforts by manufacturers to keep the ice cream buyer interested. Per person consumption has been stagnant at best in recent years, so they feel a constant need to reengage, to find new ways of exciting the consumer, especially those who have aged out of their childhood favorites. These days, the buzz words are "functional benefits," with ice creams—and other foods as well—marketed as good for the consumer in some specific way. With probiotics, for example, or extra protein. Snow Monkey promotes their Vegan Matcha Green Tea flavor as high in antioxidants, calling matcha "one of the most powerful superfoods in the jungle." Peekaboo brand is sold as the ice cream with hidden vegetables—cauliflower in the chocolate; zucchini in birthday cake flavored Unicorn, cookie dough, and vanilla; beets in cotton candy; spinach in mint chip; and carrots in strawberry. The company touts it as "indulgent ice cream that also delivers vitamins and minerals from immunity-boosting organic veggies." Killer Creamery targets its ice cream at followers of the keto diet. Nightfood is marketed as sleep-friendly, formulated not to interfere with sleep for those who like a little ice cream before bed.

Jerry Greenfield says, while the specifics may be new, he's seen this sort of thing before: "Over the course of the forty-two years of Ben & Jerry's, frozen yogurt has come and gone, and come and gone, and come and gone. So-called lite ice cream, which was a lower butterfat ice cream, lower calorie, has come and gone, and come and gone, and come and gone. And when they come, they always cut into the sales and consumption of traditional ice cream. And then they go. And it's generally because they don't taste as good. In my experience, people continue to come back to the euphoric taste of high-quality ice cream."

Vanilla Custard and Ice Cream

From Judy Herrell of Herrell's Ice Cream in Northampton, Massachusetts

Custard is made with egg yolk and is often, but not always, smoother and denser than ice cream. This recipe can be made without the egg yolks by adding ¼ tsp. guar gum and eliminating the egg. This will change the product from custard to ice cream. This basic vanilla can be made as Sweet Cream or a simple base by eliminating the vanilla extract. There are two kinds of ice cream makers for home use, electric and hand crank. Double this recipe for hand crank units.

Ingredients:

- 2 cups heavy cream
- 1 cup half & half
- ½ cup sugar
- ½ tsp. salt
- 6 large egg yolks
- ½ tsp. pure vanilla extract

Directions

- If using a freezer cannister machine, place ice cream canister into the rear of your freezer at least 24 hours ahead of time to freeze the liquid in the unit. Make sure you cannot hear sloshing when you're ready for ice cream making. Keep frozen until ready to pour in, mix, and freeze.

- Place egg yolks in a bowl and whisk until smooth. In medium saucepan over low/medium heat, warm the other ingredients, stirring consistently. Add ½ warm milk mixture into the egg yolks and stir well. Then add yolks back into saucepan. Stir constantly, being sure to scrape from the bottom if needed until the mixture will coat a spoon (170 degrees). Allow mixture to cool, pour into bowl, and cover. Place this in the refrigerator overnight.

- Assemble the ice cream maker, gently stir the cold mix, and pour it into the freezer canister. Place dasher in place, close, and turn on or crank. Freeze to soft serve consistency (hand crank will take about 20 minutes with slow cranking, electric units may freeze a bit quicker). Remove, quickly cover, and place in rear part of freezer for 3 to 4 hours before serving.

- Flavor to taste. Remember, some fruits and alcohol will make the ice cream softer because of their natural sugars.

Acknowledgements

★ ★

First, thank you to all of the food professionals, both well-known and unsung, who were so generous with their time, knowledge, and access, especially as their industry was being rocked by the COVID-19 pandemic. Thank you as well to the many authors, journalists, critics, and academics who were so gracious in sharing their time, their work, and their accumulated knowledge.

There is no way to list everyone who contributed to this project, but I do want to single out a few.

First, my wife Roberta, whose encouragement and support made this project possible. And whose wise counsel and excellent editing made the work so much better. As did the support and keen proofreading of my daughter Hannah, soon to have a Columbia University MFA that proves she is a better writer than her old man.

Thanks to author, journalist, and friend Martin Fletcher for his great advice and feedback to a first-time author. And to, among so many others, Gustavo Arellano, Marisa Baggett, Dawn Balaban, Gary Balaban, Ryan Bu, Adam Caslow, George Chen, Greg Ehresman, Carrie Ehresman, Niki Russ Federman, Paul Freedman, Tony Gemignani, Emily Gindi, Jerry Greenfield, Marvin Lender, Adrian Miller, Brad Orrison, Linda Orrison, Jennifer Pesqueira, David Portalatin, José Ralat, Yi "Mia" Shang, Josh Russ Tupper, Michael Twitty, Robb Walsh, and Psyche Williams-Forson.

And thanks to remarkable reporter Penelope Overton, and to all of the other talented journalists who helped me with elements of the book all across the country: Robert Bear, Sarah Bogaards,

Blake Douglas, Heather King, Adam Kurtz, Sarah McKinnis, Kim Mueller, Annie Pentilla, Gina Ruggeri, Frank Sabatini Jr., Natalie Saenz, Anna Szolwinski, Akhira Umar, Naomi Sakovics, and Amelia Williams.

I also want to note the sad passing of three remarkable people who had taken the time to talk with me: Cecilia Chiang, perhaps the most influential figure in the development of Chinese food in America; Mike, Mills, three-time Grand Champion at the Memphis in May barbecue competition; and world champion pizza maker Shawn Randazzo.

Finally, thank you to Chris McKenney, Hugo Villabona, Yaddyra Peralta, Hannah Jorstad Paulsen, Geena El-Haj, Minerve Jean, Morgane Leoni, and the other great pros at Mango Publishing for providing me this opportunity and so deftly nurturing and improving my work.

About the Author

Two-time Emmy winner **David Page** changed the world of food television by creating, developing, and executive-producing the groundbreaking show *Diners, Drive-Ins and Dives*. Before that, as a network news producer based in London, Frankfurt, and Budapest, he traveled Europe, Africa, and the Middle East doing two things: covering some of the biggest stories in the world and developing a passion for some of the world's most incredible food.

Page walked through Checkpoint Charlie into East Berlin the night the Berlin wall opened, but his favorite memory of the eastern side before reunification remains the weisswurst sold under the S-Bahn elevated train. He was first served couscous by Moammar Khaddafy's kitchen staff while waiting in a tent to interview the dictator in Libya. Blood oranges at a three o'clock breakfast with Yasser Arafat. Wild boar prosciutto in Rome. Bouillabaisse in Marseille. Cheese pies in Tbilisi. Venison in Salzburg. Nonstop caviar in Moscow. He even managed to slip a few food features in between the headline stories, such as a profile of Germany's leading food critic, which turned out not to be the oxymoron one might assume.

Once back in the states, Page has pursued his passion both personally and professionally. Show-producing *Good Morning America*, he was involved in a substantial amount of food coverage, including cooking segments by Emeril Lagasse. Creating *Diners, Drive-Ins and Dives* and hands-on producing its first eleven seasons took him deep into the world of American food—its vast variations, its history, its evolution, and especially the dedicated cooks and chefs keeping it vibrant. His next series, the syndicated *Beer Geeks*, dove deep into the intersection of great beer and great food. It is those experiences, that education, and the discovery of little-known stories and facts that led Page to dig even deeper and tie the strands together in *Food Americana*.

Mango Publishing, established in 2014, publishes an eclectic list of books by diverse authors—both new and established voices—on topics ranging from business, personal growth, women's empowerment, LGBTQ studies, health, and spirituality to history, popular culture, time management, decluttering, lifestyle, mental wellness, aging, and sustainable living. We were recently named 2019 *and* 2020's #1 fastest growing independent publisher by *Publishers Weekly*. Our success is driven by our main goal, which is to publish high-quality books that will entertain readers as well as make a positive difference in their lives.

Our readers are our most important resource; we value your input, suggestions, and ideas. We'd love to hear from you—after all, we are publishing books for you!

Please stay in touch with us and follow us at:

Facebook: Mango Publishing
Twitter: @MangoPublishing
Instagram: @MangoPublishing
LinkedIn: Mango Publishing
Pinterest: Mango Publishing
Newsletter: mangopublishinggroup.com/newsletter

Join us on Mango's journey to reinvent publishing, one book at a time.